THE TASTE OF
THAILAND
VATCHARIN BHUMICHITR

สวัสดี.

คุณ แม่ ที่ควรรัก.

For my mother

THE TASTE OF
THAILAND
VATCHARIN BHUMICHITR

Food photography by Clive Streeter

Specially commissioned location photography
by Michael Freeman

PAVILION

This edition published in Great Britain in 1998 by
PAVILLION BOOKS LIMITED
London House, Great Eastern Wharf
Parkgate Road, London SW11 4NQ

First published in 1988

Text copyright © Vatcharin Bhumichitr 1988
Recipe photographs (by Clive Streeter)
copyright © Pavilion Books Ltd 1988
Line illustrations (by Jane Evans)
copyright © Pavilion Books Ltd 1988
Location photographs copyright © Michael Freeman 1988
For other photographic acknowledgements
see page 220

Designed by Andrew Barron Associates

British Cataloguing in Publication Data
Bhumichitr, Vatcharin
The taste of Thailand.
1. Cookery, Thai
I. Title
641'.59593   TX724.5.T5

ISBN 1 86205 009 0

2 4 6 8 10 9 7 5 3 1

Printed and bound in Singapore
by Kyodo

Photograph on pages 2/3: Detail from the entrance doors
of the Temple Wat Phra That Haripunchai
page 6: Chiang Mai at dawn, mist from the northern
mountains

CONTENTS

Introduction 12

From Siam to Thailand 17
A brief history

House and Market 27
An introduction to Thai cooking,
essential equipment, ingredients
and techniques, drinks.
How to use this book. Measurements

Reflections in a Field of Water 45
Country cooking.
First stages and elementary dishes

City of Angels 65
Bangkok life. More advanced food

By the Sea 101
Seafood

Up Country 125
Food from the Northern Regions of Thailand

Rites of Passage 149
Food for special occasions. Thai fruits.
Thai desserts. Vegetable carving

Eating out 179
A personal choice of some of Thailand's many
restaurants with a selection of recipes

Glossary 211

Recipe Index 212

Main Index 217

*Khao Sam Lawy
Yod National Park,
Southern Thailand*

INTRODUCTION

*Previous pages:
Scenes from town
life in old Siam:
making music,
offering food,
chewing betel nut.
A mural in Wat
Mongkut, Bangkok*

The taste of Thai cooking is easy to identify: lemon grass and fish sauce, coriander, galangal, garlic, sweet basil and coconut milk all combine to make a harmony that is unforgettable. As is the look of the food: set out in a group of small dishes on which the ingredients have been decoratively arranged, with vegetables carved as flowers, fish and meat arranged in neat patterns, tiny bowls of clear soup steaming beside a communal pot of fluffy rice. Surprisingly, it has taken a long time for Thai cuisine to reach the West but now it has, the growth in its popularity seems unstoppable, with restaurants opening in the major cities of Europe and America almost daily. Partially it is Thailand's geographical location, reflected in its food, at a point half way between India and China that must appeal to the Western palate. But it is also the lightness of the food and the way it corresponds to recent nutritional thinking that has made it so popular: meat, always without fat, makes up only a small proportion of a Thai meal, the largest element being quickly cooked vegetables that remain firm with all their flavours preserved. Thai food is seldom cooked for long and is always fresh.

Every Thai is interested in food. Because we believe that life should be *Sanuk* or fun, the pleasures of eating are very important to us. Preparing food well and serving it beautifully is never a chore, perhaps because much of Thai cooking is very straightforward. Few dishes take longer than eight to twelve minutes to cook. A Thai meal allows the chef considerable style without having to disappear into a kitchen all evening – we love to have guests in Thailand but we like to be with them, not somewhere out of sight.

The good news for those wishing to make our food is that even the more sophisticated dishes photographed in this book will not involve an arduous programme of cordon-bleu-style cookery lessons. This book has been carefully graded so that you can begin with one or two elementary dishes yet soon be able to set out a full Thai meal with all its unique flavours. The other good news is that you need buy only a few special ingredients in order to start at once: the average modern cook has most of the basics to hand as well as the equipment needed so this will not be a costly exercise. Happily, Thai cooking is about flavours and methods, and not about rituals, and these methods can be applied to whatever ingredients are available locally. Our country is often called the crossroads of Asia, and we are very open to outside influences and love to experiment, so if you cannot get oriental vegetables then use whatever seems the nearest local equivalent, any Thai cook would do the same quite happily.

It is the range and adaptability of Thai cooking that raises it beyond the level of just another local cuisine. All occasions, private and public, all ceremonies, all the important moments in our lives have food somewhere at the heart of them. Offering food to a monk in his saffron robes during the morning alms gathering makes food an essential component of our religious faith. Visitors are often amazed at the lengths we go to in our search for the unusual – on the outskirts of the city of Korat is an unattractive concrete building which appears to be mainly a garage during the day, but at night it is a restaurant whose speciality is the most wonderful duck. Scruffy it may be, but rich businessmen and well-dressed women are not averse to putting up with its drawbacks for the pleasure of its food.

One word of warning, Thai food is addictive, you may not want to eat Thai food every day but you will certainly want to return to it often. When I first came to London as a student in 1976 this was a problem as it was virtually impossible to find even those few essential ingredients that give Thai food its special character. There were four Thai restaurants in London struggling to serve a facsimile of our cuisine, but even so it was easier to give up the idea of eating Thai and settle for a Chinese

Village at early morning. The traditional offering of food to passing monks

meal. Of course we went on trying to conjure up echoes of home in our flats and bedsits and the arrival of a visitor from Bangkok with a fresh supply of raw materials would be the excuse for a party. It was a visit to my brother in Chicago that showed me a different lifestyle, for there, as in New York and Los Angeles, a large Thai community had led to the setting up not only of authentic restaurants but also of supermarkets with everything a Thai cook needs. While I was still a student the great surge in tourism to the Far East brought with it a wide public keen to find again the food they had enjoyed on holiday. It began to look as if that American experience could be repeated in London.

Part of my family are hotel owners and restaurateurs and I had worked with them before I left for England. They agreed that I should test my theory and when my studies were over I opened a shop selling Thai produce. The results were electric, not only did addicts both Thai and British flock to buy the sauces and fresh vegetables flown in every week, but suddenly rivals were springing up all around. Enough of shops I thought, it's time to really produce the food and so I opened the Chiang Mai restaurant in Soho determined to be among the first to prove that Thai food outside Thailand could be absolutely authentic. I began by doing much of the cooking myself and have gradually trained a band of helpers with myself on hand to ensure that there are no lazy concessions to some mythical notion of Western taste. I'm happy to say that for some time now the restaurant has been the only Thai establishment in the *Michelin Guide*, and the *Good Food Guide* has said that the Chiang Mai is among those responsible for the renaissance of Soho as a culinary centre. This book is a response to the requests of those who regularly come to the Chiang Mai and ask me to recommend a practical guide to cooking Thai meals at home. Because of the intimate relationship between Thai life and the way we eat, each chapter takes a look at an aspect of the country and the food that comes from it so that the meals you are making will have a context. There is food that a rice farmer or fisherman might enjoy and there's special food for great festivals and royal occasions. I have tried to create a portrait of a people who consider their cuisine to be an art, a ceremony, an offering.

To help ensure that everything works, I enlisted the support of a friend, Jackie Hunt, who undertook to learn from scratch how Thai cuisine operates. Jackie's mother was a professional cook and Jackie first encountered Thai food in America where she lived for seven years, so she has been also able to translate my recipes for the American kitchen. Jackie has watched me cook all the dishes here, has noted everything down then gone off to try for herself. We have eaten a great deal of Thai food over the past year!

So please give it a try. We start with the equipment and ingredients you'll need along with some advice on techniques, but from then on it's a steady progression of dishes, from elementary to fairly complex; just go as far as you wish. We Thais are very individualistic and easy-going in our cooking and when you have learned the basic rules you can vary the taste to suit your own palate, a little sweeter or a little more savoury, hotter or milder, it is up to you. My hope is that with the aid of my book you will find that your meals are a little more *Sanuk*.

Dusk. Thara, near Krabi, Southern Thailand

FROM SIAM
TO THAILAND

A BRIEF HISTORY

A colossal statue of the Buddha smiles serenely from the shadows of a ruined temple, its walls overhung with tropical vegetation. There is an echo of clicking cameras and a party of tourists shuffles back onto their coach. In under an hour they will have been whisked in air-conditioned luxury from this image of ageless beauty to the honking nightmare of Bangkok's rush-hour traffic. When they return home they will take away a jumble of memories: straw-hatted peasants bending to tend their rice in a flooded paddy, soaring sky-scraper banks, a fairy-tale royal palace with gilded roofs, bustling markets where they were offered anything from grilled squid to an imitation Gucci bag. Before they came they probably had nothing more than a few misconceptions gleaned from Yul Brynner in *The King and I*; but when they leave they will have experienced contradictions so strong few can begin to reconcile them.

Thailand is not a very big nor a very rich country, but it is unique. It has a way of life that mixes ancient ritual with the ways of the modern world. Culture shock is everywhere: the Buddhist monk in his traditional robes rides pillion on a Japanese motor-bike, on the wall of a room whirring with computers hangs a shrine pungent with incense on which offerings of food have been laid. The contradictions are in the very environment: spectacular scenery vies with squalid slums, delicate stuccoed temples are overshadowed by the modernist concrete headquarters of multinational corporations. We have a centuries old Asian culture yet we turn willingly to the West for the latest fads and fashions. Sometimes it's hard, even for a Thai, to work out how this works and where it is going next.

Thailand is the central country of South East Asia, on the edge of what used to be French Indo-China. We have Burma to the west, Laos to the north, our querulous neighbour Cambodia to the east, to the south lies Malaysia. Although we have much in common with our neighbours we Thais are different. Our ancestors moved out of central and southern China about the ninth century possibly as a result of the Mongol invasions. At first they crossed Cambodia and entered the eastern part of what is now our country where they were subservient to the ruling Khmer empire. By the thirteenth century the Thai population was large enough to rebel against its distant Khmer rulers in their capital at Angkor Wat and to set up an independent kingdom centred on the city of Sukhothai which means, appropriately, the Dawn of Happiness.

Engraving of a Siamese war elephant

Previous page: King Mongkut of Siam (Rama IV), in ceremonial dress, the author's distant ancestor

A Bangkok postman of 1911. The mail was reputedly the most efficient government service at the time

Sukhothai occupied a site at the very centre of the great plain divided by the mighty Chao Phya River, a great thoroughfare which provided the canals and channels for the paddy fields that were, and still are, the wealth of the nation. At Sukhothai our culture was formed, our unique architecture came into being, and Buddhist monks from Sri Lanka and Hindu Brahmins from India came as teachers. A blending of these two faiths gave us our unique state religion based on the person of the monarch that still exists today. King Ramkamhaeng, the second ruler of Sukhothai, gave us an alphabet freeing us from the limitations of pictograms.

But our history has also been marked by almost perpetual crises. Wars with our neighbours led to successive invasions and eventually the Sukhothai period ended with the removal of the capital to the more southerly site of Ayuthya, another great city only an hour's drive from modern Bangkok. For four hundred years this city of elegant spires, gilded Buddhas, sumptuous royal palaces was one of the wonders of the East, but in 1767 calamity struck: after a two-week seige an invading Burmese army succeeded in breaching the city walls and in an

Previous page:
Giant statue of the
Buddha among the
ruins of Sukhothai,
central Thailand

orgy of looting and burning reduced Ayuthya to rubble and wiped out the royal family. The Thai nation seemed to be finished.

Our saviour was a Chinese General called Taksin who, seeing that the city and indeed the country was lost, rallied a group of soldiers and retreated down the Chao Phya River to its estuary. Crossing the river he set up camp at Thonburi where refugees from the burning capital could gather. There, modern Siam was born. When he felt he had trained enough men this brilliant general gradually drove the Burmese from the country, attempting to salvage what he could of the shattered nation. Sadly, as his reign progressed, it became clear that his sanity was slipping away and eventually his courtiers were forced to end his life. His successor Chao Phya Chakri, a Thai, became the first ruler from the dynasty that still reigns over our country. He established his new capital across the river at a place that foreigners knew as Bangkok but which we call Krung Thep, the City of Angels.

The Chakri dynasty has been extraordinary. Its first three kings rebuilt the country, painstakingly reconstructing the art, architecture, poetry, and music of Ayuthaya. They extended their authority north, to the ancient Kingdom of Chiang Mai, giving us access to the high mountain peaks of the Golden Triangle and bringing other peoples, the hill tribes, within our nation, and south into the narrow strip of territory bordered on the east by the Gulf of Thailand and on the west by the Andaman Sea. Thus the map of our country came to look like the head of an elephant – our national symbol – the great spaces of the east stretching towards Laos being the ear while that narrow isthmus to the south is the trunk.

Succeeding monarchs struggled successfully to ward off both the French and the British in their manoeuvres to annex our land into their neighbouring empires, modernizing the country on Western lines so that we could remain independent.

*Modern re-
enactment near
Surin, of an ancient
battle between the
Burmese and the
Thais*

Thailand's first National Assembly, the building was designed by an Italian architect in the 1930s. Here it is illuminated for the King's birthday

King Mongkut and his son King Chulalongkorn introduced an astonishing range of Western ideas from railways to universities and despatched young Thais abroad to learn from the best teachers available. Thus in the twentieth century political movements began that were inspired by the idea that Siam should have a parliament. In 1932 a bloodless coup ended the absolute power of the monarchy, and the name of the country was subsequently changed from Siam to Thailand, or 'land of the free', though this did not lead to immediate democracy. Our subsequent history was one of successive military regimes, though it must be said that these were not as bad as that may sound to an outsider. The Thai military is a vast and

Top: Gilded roofs of the Grand Palace, Bangkok. Left: Intricate, inlaid sculpture of Hanuman, the Monkey King, on the walls of the Grand Palace

complicated national institution with many families having at least one member involved. In a way it is almost a civil service as much as a fighting force and it ran the country fairly well. However, there has been considerable pressure for change in recent years and at last we now have an elected parliament even if many politicians are still soldiers in suits.

In recent times our national traumas have been occupation by the Japanese during the Second World War (with the building of the infamous Bridge over the River Kwai a short distance from Bangkok), and more recently the Vietnam War which led to Thailand being the main Rest and Recreation centre for American troops which turned areas of our major cities into

*H.M. King
Bhumiphol
Adulyadej Rama IX,
a twentieth-century
monarch
surrounded by
ancient ceremonial*

red light districts full of strip joints and massage parlours. Somehow we have survived all this and still remain independent and unique. Statistically we are poor, with appalling slums spreading around Bangkok as people are drawn to the boom city in search of illusory wealth, and yet it *is* a boom city with businesses flourishing and a growing middle class.

Despite all the problems of the modern world Thailand still has much of old Siam. Our present King, H. M. Bhumiphol Adulyadej Rama IX, is beloved for his good works and the fact that he has tried to nurture parliamentary control of the country. Much of village life remains unchanged with peasant farmers and simple fishermen still living in the elegant wooden stilt houses favoured by their ancestors. Even in the bustling cities there is still time for the delicate calm observance of religious duty – offering food to a begging monk, taking an offering of flowers and incense to a temple.

Although the typical Thai dwelling is a wooden house by a *klong* or stream, most Thais today dream of a modern house not much different from that seen in Europe or America. How could it be otherwise? The differences between peoples are far less than the similarities. And yet, when one of us has his modern house, with all its so-called amenities, the first thing we do is call in the monks to bless it and to set up our family statue of the Buddha beside which we place the images of our ancestors and so preserve the continuum of life that has held us together as a people ever since that distant migration centuries ago.

Of course many of our national characteristics have been lost, but oddly enough what survives has done so just because it is so strong even in the face of enormous pressure from Western-style films, music, fashions, television. Where else would you find a place that celebrates the opening of a bank, equipped with all the latest computerized technology, with the simultaneous opening of a model home, in traditional style, designed to house the dispossessed spirit of the land whose anger might result in all sorts of dreadful calamities? In any case, a mere half-hour's drive from Bangkok where the dying light plays on the flooded ricefields and a smiling child rides his tame water-buffalo home to his village, there is still a world of calm and wisdom unspoiled by the city dwellers' folly, where as the evening meal is set out and thanks are given for the blessings of the rice harvest that sustains rich and poor alike there is still that sense of community and dignity that the East has always cherished.

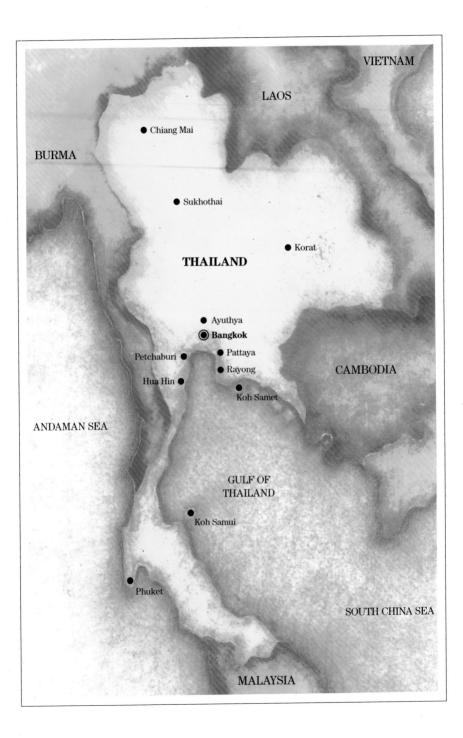

HOUSE & MARKET

AN INTRODUCTION TO THAI COOKING.
ESSENTIAL EQUIPMENT, INGREDIENTS
AND TECHNIQUES, DRINKS.
HOW TO USE THIS BOOK. MEASUREMENTS.

When I was a schoolboy we lived in Saladaeng, then a pleasant tree-lined suburb on the outskirts of Bangkok beside which ran the Sathorn Klong or canal. In those days it was still possible to see flat-bottomed boats going to and from the Chao Phya River, then the city's main thoroughfare. Our house, like others in the neighbourhood, stood in its own garden, a two-storey brick and wood structure with an outside staircase to the first floor veranda in what was called the 'colonial' style because the fashion for such houses grew in the Chinese business community whose associates in Malaya had acquired a taste for the lifestyle of the British officials and settlers. It was a handsome building but despite its 'modern' look it had much in common with the traditional Thai stilt houses in the bright green paddy fields that were then only a short distance away from the city. Just like her country cousins, our cook, Kuhn Aat, worked in a wooden outhouse, sitting cross-legged on the ground as she chopped and sliced the vegetables or pounded the spices in a heavy stone mortar before tossing them all into the sizzling wok on the earthenware charcoal stove. My mother would prepare special dishes like *Nam Prik*, a pungent shrimp paste sauce that we all loved and which every Thai cook prepares in her own way, some adding baby eggplant, others adding more chilli. Mother saw to the presentation of the food, the decorative details and in all essentials, this was Thai cuisine as it had been for centuries, in equipment, methods

19th century engraving of Thai ladies enjoying a meal

and of course tastes. Today, in the countless hamlets that dot the Thai countryside, the old methods are still in use and when faced with this image of the traditional kitchen, with its ceramic bowls and wooden implements, the newcomer to Thai cooking may feel that this is all too removed from the realities of contemporary life. Until the Sixties this might have been so, but now Bangkok has changed – our 'colonial' house was pulled down twenty years ago and replaced by a modern concrete building, the sort of dwelling you see everywhere now. Open any Thai magazine and you'll see advertisements for the Ideal Home our young marrieds dream about, identical to the sort of suburban villas the middle classes want everywhere. We may deplore this standardization but then we don't have to squat on an earthen floor or cook on a charcoal brazier. At first our new home meant little difference to the food. We still had an outhouse and Kuhn Aat went on cooking much as before. The sparkling fitted-kitchen, with its cabinets, its refrigerator and gas cooker was initially more for display

Page 26: Floating market. Once to be found everywhere, such markets are gradually becoming less common

than use, but gradually reality caught up with us. First the rice was no longer cooked in the traditional way, a new Japanese electric rice-cooker saw to that. And then, as Kuhn Aat got older and those who might have taken her place were now finding work in the new hotels and factories of our booming economy, the family began to find that the modern kitchen was more and more suited to their needs. Thai cookery had imperceptibly entered the twentieth century. When I was last in Bangkok Kuhn Aat was so old she only made our favourite dishes for special occasions, the bulk of the meal was made by the daughters of the house. Most of our once substantial garden had been sold off and built on and near our front gate was a small restaurant, that sent in food when requested. Our *klong* is now an invisible channel bordered by two thundering expressways, and the few 'colonial' houses that are left are being transformed into restaurants that offer a nostalgic glimpse of old Bangkok for those who remember it. No, you will find little difficulty in cooking Thai food in a modern kitchen, we got there first.

The Thai ideal home of today advertised on a hoarding on the outskirts of Chiang Mai

Overleaf: The traditional kitchen in the northern stilthouse in the Old Chiang Mai cultural centre

ESSENTIAL EQUIPMENT

Details of a traditional kitchen, though easy to reproduce in the west

Any large frying pan or skillet will do, but if you are planning to cook oriental food regularly it would be sensible to buy a wok – or even two.

A saucepan with a tight lid is needed for cooking rice, but again a moderate outlay will get an electric rice-cooker, which is easy to use, makes perfect rice and then keeps it warm for up to five hours. Highly recommended.

A pestle and mortar is used in all Thai kitchens; very often two of different weights (a stone one for obtaining a really thoroughly-pounded blend, and a wooden one for a more gentle mixture). But a blender or food processor can also be used for most dishes, and a coffee-grinder is needed for finely grinding spices for curried dishes.

Many older cooks may have a steamer of some sort, and large pans are available that have a steaming section. You can, of course,

use the Chinese bamboo steamers which can be bought in most oriental stores and specialist sections of department stores. For some dishes, you can use an upturned bowl in a large saucepan of water to support a plate of food for steaming.

A coarse mesh long-handled strainer is also necessary for scooping food from the deep-fryer, dipping noodles etc. They come in various sizes from Chinese and oriental stores. In some instances a slotted spoon could be substituted.

Apart from these, you only need what any well-equipped kitchen should have: saucepans, a chopping board, a mincer or grinder for meat, a pan for deep-frying and the usual range of kitchen knives, though if you plan to cook Thai food often you may find it practical to buy a heavy Chinese chopping 'axe' and a thin, ultra-sharp knife for carving fruit and vegetables.

While kitchen equipment may present few problems, it has always been the lack of authentic ingredients that has stood in the way of producing real Thai food in the West. At home, our nearby market, although small, was a treasure-house of vegetables and spices, of pungent pastes and snowy white noodles, of pickles and herbs. And that local arcade was only an echo of the great Ba Klong Dalat market on the banks of the Chao Phya River in the heart of the city. At its jetty dozens of flat-bottomed boats would unload the produce of the farms and villages in the city's hinterland. Today, travel by water is less important than it was twenty years ago, and it is in the streets at the entrance to Ba Klong Dalat that you now find all the morning bustle of lorries arriving piled high with cabbages and sweet potatoes, with durian and baby corn, with fish and poultry.

Inside, the market is like a vast wooden galleon turned upside down, the high pitched roof is criss-crossed with wooden beams from which tiny fans turn like propellers out of water. Below is a riot of every conceivable gift of the countryside and yet there is order – the Thai love of pattern ensures that the market women pile their produce in decorative shapes: a fan of silvery fish, a pyramid of emerald cabbages, neat knots of long beans. At the centre of the market, under a shaft of sunlight from an opening in the roof, is the gilded shrine to one of our kings whose shadowy statuette is hard to identify. I remember asking one of the elderly market women who it was but she only knew him as 'the grandfather who owns the country', a charming and not inexact description of our earlier monarchs. Today the market porters honour this venerable figure with gifts of fresh coconut milk. Striped plastic straws stick out of the lopped heads of the coconuts; a mix of the rustic and the modern that is very Bangkok. These porters are hard-working, aggressive characters who manipulate their trolleys with an alarming dexterity, hissing behind you to warn you to clear out of their way and hurtling by so close you always feel that this is the time your ankle will get a nasty crack. The market women have to keep a sharp look out, if they turn away for an instant a passing hand will snatch at a mango and be off before they notice.

The market is home to a tribe of happy cats that bask in its shadiness and feast on the limitless leftovers. In fact all Thai markets are also restaurants with food stalls fringing the entrances where workers and shoppers can squat on low stools and eat what is of course the freshest meal imaginable. If you really want to eat well in Thailand haunt the markets, sample a skewer of grilled satay from one stall, some Kai Pa Lo, pork and egg in a rich sauce, or Gaeng Pet, a curry, from another then a sweet pancake with freshly grated coconut to finish. The surrounding bustle provides the cabaret.

Of course, no one can pretend that this abundance can be found outside Asia, the smelly heaps of purple shrimp-paste, the bulging jars of pickled garlic cloves, the tanks of wriggling exotic fish, the deep ochre cart-

A highspeed porter outside Ba Klong Dalat food market, Bangkok

wheels of preserved fruit are all unique to the East. But much of what you will need is now available, sometimes from a shop specializing in Thai produce or from Chinese, Indian or other oriental stores, and even from some of the larger supermarket chains. Meat and poultry are much the same anywhere, as is most seafood, though later I'll suggest alternative fish to those available only in the East. Again, with vegetables there are fewer problems than once, and today some once rare plants can be found, not only in Chinese shops, but increasingly in the smarter supermarkets and the food halls of department stores.

While you can substitute fish and vegetables for local varieties, the unchangeable heart of Thai cuisine is the body of spices, herbs and roots that give it its unique taste. These you must search out in Thai, Chinese or Indian stores, though you can begin with far fewer than you might fear.

BASIC INGREDIENTS

The following ten ingredients are essential for Thai cookery and you should buy them before you start on the recipes in the following chapter.

Chillies Small red, small green, long red, long green, and some fatter than others. Which to buy? A general rule might be the smaller the hotter. Very small chillies (½-1 in/1-2.5 cm) are only found in specialist stores, the slightly larger (1-2 in/2.5-4 cm) can be found in most Chinese, Asian and similar stores, and the much longer varieties can sometimes be found in supermarkets. The longest are perhaps a little milder, but will still be fiery. In the restaurant we test each batch for their strength, but this takes the palate, and enthusiasm, of a connoisseur. The recipes given are geared to 'medium' pungency and you may adjust up or down according to taste.

Do remember that all chillies, including dried, need to be handled with great care. Not only the skin but the seeds contain the hot oil, and a careless wipe of the eye while chopping chillies can cause a great deal of discomfort. So wash your hands thoroughly after using them and under no circumstances touch any part of your face, particularly the delicate skin around the eyes.

Dried chillies are usually the long red variety and are used here in some recipes.

Chilli powder is powdered chilli with no other additives and is readily available.

Coconut Coconut milk can be prepared from fresh coconut, dessicated coconut, powdered coconut, and coconut block. It is also available in cans. The best is prepared from fresh coconut flesh which, in the US, can be found frozen, but very good results can be obtained from unsweetened dessicated coconut (see below). Coconut powder is usually in small foil packets and can be found in most Chinese and oriental stores – follow the instructions on the packet. Coconut cream in blocks is available in many supermarkets and stores, as are cans of coconut milk. These are perhaps the most convenient to use as you will find that the cream and thin milk have already separated.

To make coconut milk from fresh or dessicated flesh, pour hot water over a given amount of coconut in a bowl and let it stand for about 15 minutes. Pour the mixture through a muslin-lined sieve into a container: gather up the corners of the muslin and squeeze out the remaining liquid. This is thick coconut milk and if you refrigerate it for a little while a thick cream will rise to the top which can be spooned off. Thin coconut milk is obtained by repeating the process with the once-used flesh; a second pressing.

Coconut	+	Liquid	=	Coconut milk
8 oz/230 g		30 fl.oz/855 ml		20 fl.oz/570 ml

This can also be frozen successfully.

To make coconut milk from a block, add 6 fl oz/175 ml hot water to 3 oz/90 g coconut. Stir until dissolved. This should give approximately 8 fl oz/240 ml coconut milk,

Coriander (Chinese Parsley, Cilantro) Coriander is used extensively as a flavouring, and as a garnish. The root is also used, often pounded with garlic and other ingredients to make a marinade. Leaf and root are bought complete. In the West the roots are often cut short and so must be used with an inch or so of the leaf stalk. After rinsing and drying, the roots will keep in a sealed container in a refrigerator for several days. Coriander is now readily available in supermarkets and stores as well as in specialist shops.

The seeds are used in curry pastes.

Fish Sauce, Fish Gravy This is the basic savoury flavour of Thai cooking for which there is *no* substitute. Available bottled in Chinese and oriental stores. It is made from fermented fish or seafood and imparts a very distinctive flavour. It is quite salty. There are several varieties: anchovy, prawn, fish, squid, with some variation in strength, colour and thus flavour, according to brand. Obviously, if you find you have bought a strongly-flavoured variety you will have to modify the amount you use.

Opposite: Typical Thai herbs and vegetables: coriander, lime leaf, purple aubergine, taro, green papaya, bitter melon, ginger, shallot, pea aubergine, lemon grass, garlic flower, yellow chilli, krachai, galangal, kaffir lime, white aubergine, wing bean, long bean, red chilli

Garlic cloves with bundles of young bamboo

Garlic Indispensable in Thai cooking. The Asian variety is much smaller than that usual in Europe and the recipes have assumed the use of the European. While many people use garlic crushers, I much prefer to chop the cloves finely by hand. Pickled garlic can be bought pre-prepared in jars, but there is a recipe to make your own on p. 98.

Lemon Grass Again, an indispensible part of Thai cuisine. The stalks are bought in bundles of about 6-8 and are usually 7-8 in/18-20 cm long. The ends are trimmed and the stalk finely sliced. One average stalk will give approximately 3 tbs/45 ml finely sliced lemon grass. The stalks will last quite well for 2-3 weeks in a refrigerator, and chopped lemon grass can be put in a plastic bag and frozen. Chopped lemon grass is also available dried in small packets.

Lime Leaves These are the dark green glossy leaves of the Kaffir lime and impart a pungent lemon-lime flavour. They are available in some oriental stores and are worth looking for – they are usually packaged as small branches in a plastic bag. They keep well and, of course, can be frozen. They are also available dried. Slicing is best achieved by using kitchen scissors to cut fine strips of the leaf.

Oil I have not specified any particular oil, and almost any vegetable oil will serve, except olive oil which imparts a flavour quite foreign to Thai dishes. Normally I prefer to use peanut, soy, safflower or sunflower oils. Most Thai recipes begin by frying garlic in the oil to flavour it.

Pepper These recipes call for either ground white or black pepper. One recipe calls for fresh green peppercorns, which are the un-dried sprigs of pepper berries, but black peppercorns may be substituted.

Soy Sauce I have made a distinction between 'light' and 'dark' soy sauce, the dark being slightly thicker, sweeter, and usually a little more expensive. It is used as much to add a little colour to a dish as for flavour.

Kaffir lime leaf

The following ingredients are used less often and need only be bought for special recipes. There are rarer ingredients, used only once or twice in the book; these are explained when they appear.

Pea aubergines

Aubergine or Eggplant In Thailand, we use varieties of eggplant not easily available in Europe or the US. The pea aubergine is, as its name suggests, the size of a pea or small marble, and the small green aubergine is about 1 in/2.5 cm in diameter. These can be found in some Chinese and specialist stores. Otherwise the yellow and black aubergines commonly found outside Asia may be substituted, cut down to the size of the green aubergine.

Banana Leaf This can be obtained in some oriental stores. We use it to make containers for steaming. The dishes which call for banana leaf containers may be cooked in individual bowls, instead.

Banana leaf

Basil, Holy and Sweet Fresh holy basil can be bought in oriental stores and is also available dried. It has a darker leaf than the European basil and a slightly aniseed, sharper flavour. If you are unable to find it, sweet basil may be substituted.

Bean Curd This can be bought in oriental stores, health food stores, and some supermarkets. It is usually in blocks of approximately 4 oz/100 g (and multiples) in its liquid, which is discarded. A 4 oz/100 g block will give 4 × 1 in/2.5 cm cubes. It is very delicate and won't last more than a couple of days in the refrigerator.

Fried bean curd is available pre-prepared in oriental stores.

Bean Curd Sheets These are bought dried in packets from oriental stores. They look rather like wrinkled brown paper and are extremely delicate in their dry state. To use them for

Bean curd sheet

wrapping they have to be soaked for 5-6 minutes to soften them, and while they tear easily, you can 'patch' with other pieces.

Red Bean Curd is available in 8 oz/230 g jars.

Bean Sauce Black bean, yellow bean and red bean sauces are equally salty and flavourful, and interchangeable: choice often depends on what would look more attractive in the dish. All are made from preserved soy beans and are usually available in bottles or jars.

Curry, Paste and Powder Several kinds of paste are used in Thai cuisine and most are available pre-prepared in foil packets. But it is much more satisfactory to make your own and recipes are given on p. 92-p. 93. When curry powder is stipulated in a recipe a pre-prepared mild Indian curry powder can be used.

Krachai

Dried Shrimp An ingredient frequently used in Thai dishes, both whole and ground. It can usually be found in Chinese and oriental stores in small packets.

Galangal

Galangal (Galanga, Galangale, Kha, Laos) This looks similar to ginger root, but has a more translucent skin and a pinkish tinge. It is peeled like ginger, but sliced rather than slivered. It is available fresh in oriental stores and can also be bought dried.

Ginger Always used in fresh root form and widely available. The root is first peeled and usually sliced thin, slivered, or diced very small.

Kaffir Lime This is roughly the same size and shape as the common lime but with a knobbly skin. The skin is often used, chopped, in recipes for curry paste. The skin of the common lime may be substituted.

Krachai Also known as lesser ginger, it is of the same family as ginger and galangal, though is a smaller root. It has a fiercer, wilder flavour than ginger. Sometimes available fresh in oriental stores, it can also be found dried in small packets and in this form should be soaked in water for 30 minutes before use.

Mushrooms The dried mushrooms called for in many of these recipes are usually called Dried Black Fungus or Champignon Noir, and can be bought in 2 oz/60 g packets. Buy the smallest variety available – avoiding any that are larger and coarser. For most recipes you will only need 6-7 pieces. When they are soft and pliable they can be cut into smaller pieces. Your 2 oz/60 g packet should be enough for 8-10 dishes. Straw and oyster mushrooms can be found conveniently in cans. Some dried mushrooms contain a high proportion of sandy grit and need to be checked carefully after soaking.

Oyster Sauce This is sold in bottles and is widely available.

Peanuts Ground roasted peanuts are frequently used, and can be bought whole and ground at home. Those easiest available will probably be salted, but this does not matter.

Preserved Turnip (Chi Po) This is used only in small amounts, usually chopped fine. Found in Chinese and oriental stores.

Preserved Radish (Tang Chi) This is often found whole or in slices, in vacuum-sealed packages from Chinese or oriental stores. We use it in small amounts, slivered or chopped, to add texture and flavour.

Rice Vinegar While most white vinegars can be used, I prefer the authenticity of the rice vinegar which is readily available in all Chinese and other specialist stores.

Carrying shallots to market

Shallots These are the small red onions usually found in Chinese and similar shops. European shallots can also be used, but if neither is available a small onion can be substituted.

Shrimp Paste This can be found in jars, tins and packages. Pungent and salty, it lasts very well and is used only in small amounts.

Spring Onion/Scallion This is a frequent ingredient in Thai dishes both as a flavouring and as a garnish and sliced in many different ways to enhance the appearance of a dish.

Tamarind

Tamarind The pulp of the fruit is exported in a compressed packaged form. To extract the juice or water, the pulp should be dissolved in hot water and the resulting liquid strained. It is quite sour and if it is not available lemon juice may be substituted in twice the amount of tamarind required.

Taro This rather bland-flavoured tuber is used as a vegetable or pulped to make a dessert with flavourings.

Turmeric Another member of the ginger family, this can occasionally be found fresh in oriental stores, but is more frequently available in powdered form.

Turmeric

BASIC TECHNIQUES

Chopping chillies

Home from marketing you are ready to begin. As I said earlier, the time you will have to spend actually cooking is quite small, which is why Thai food is ideal for the Western dinner party. But there is a price to pay for this: everything does have to be prepared in advance, and that means a lot of slicing, chopping and pounding to ensure that all the ingredients are lined up ready for the quick burst of cooking that you will finally do. There is a charming myth that because knives are a sign of aggression they are never seen at a Thai meal and that is why everything has to be cut down to a size that can be eaten on a spoon with rice. I don't know whether there is any truth in this – it is probably more accurate to say that only by cutting vegetables, meat and poultry into tiny segments can you both seal in their flavours and stir-fry them quickly in the oriental manner.

Basic techniques are:

Vegetable preparation In Thailand we prefer our ingredients prepared in as delicate a way as possible. So think small. Vegetables cut finely cook quickly and thus retain the maximum amount of their essential goodness. Garlic, shallots, ginger, chillies, etc., are very finely sliced, slivered or chopped. Hard vegetables, e.g. carrots and potatoes, are cut or sliced in small pieces; green vegetables such as broccoli are cut into small florets.

Stir-frying If you have ever cooked a Chinese meal you will be familiar with this method of cooking. It is simple and fast, but requires your constant attention. As its name implies, ingredients are stirred while being cooked: the stirring is, in fact, more a matter of turning the ingredients in the cooking oil or liquid to ensure that they are exposed to the heated medium. It is best achieved in a long-handled wok over high heat since you can manipulate the cooking vessel over the heat source. It is very fast and vegetables should be cooked in this manner only for a few seconds. They should remain crisp and bright-coloured.

Steaming Many dishes are steamed and a large steamer is a good investment. Steaming is timed from the moment the dish is placed over water already boiling in the lower section of the steamer and producing steam.

STOCK/BROTH

In the restaurant and at home, I make a stock from fresh chicken carcasses or from beef or pork bones, and water. No vegetables, herbs or spices are added. The carcasses or bones are covered with water, brought to boiling point, the heat immediately reduced, the liquid skimmed of any impurities which may have come to the surface as scum, and then simmered for at least two hours, skimming from time to time as necessary.

Commercial stock cubes are full of additional flavourings and should only be used as a last resort. Use water as an alternative. Another possibility is essence of chicken if available. This essence, is in a 2½ fl oz/70 ml jar and will turn to a jelly if left in the refrigerator. While quite expensive, it is highly concentrated and can be quite heavily diluted to make a light stock: 3 tsp/15 ml per cup of water; 2 tbs/30 ml per pt/570 ml.

And so to eat. The ideal balanced Thai meal has steamed rice, small bowls of clear soup for each diner, a steamed dish and a fried dish, a strong sauce usually with chillies used as a dip for vegetables and a salad often tossed with meat or fish. Dishes are not served as separate courses, everything is set out together and eaten as each diner wishes by simply dipping his or her spoon into whichever is fancied and carrying a little back to his or her plate to be combined with the rice that has already been served there. Serving spoons are seldom used, eating is a shared matter and no one takes a large individual helping. You go on dipping in until you have had sufficient, not until you have dutifully cleared your plate. There should always be extra rice in case visitors drop in, formal invitations to dine are not usual in Thailand, and if someone comes it is thought better to run up some new dishes rather than make more of what has already been cooked – it is more *Sanuk*, that essential fun element we like so much.

Westerners who have patiently mastered the difficult art of eating with chopsticks often feel cheated when they discover that Thais only use them for eating noodles, which are of Chinese origin anyway. In the country, people often eat with their fingers, rolling the rice into a ball before dipping into the spicy flavourings. But for most of us, fork, spoon and plate are the norm. When our court was modelled on that of the Celestial Emperors, noble Thais did eat with chopsticks but when King Chulalongkorn began to modernize our country in the last century this brought not only universities and railways but also such Western fashions as long hair for women and the European style of dining. In the King's charming Victorian-style palace *The Vimanmek*, the pretty dining table is set out with French cut-glass and English porcelain stamped with the symbols of Thai royalty, and from there the habit spread.

The equipment may have changed but the form of the meal hasn't. There are no hors d'oeuvres as such but it is usual for those not involved in the cooking to have a drink, say whisky, while nibbling at snacks the returning workers have brought home with them: a little spicy sausage nibbled with cashew nuts and tiny cubes of fresh ginger and a pungent salad made from grated raw papaya tossed with fish sauce and mixed with tiny hot green chillies. To these will be added the dishes of the main meal, brought out as they are cooked so that they can be sampled with the drinks. When all the food has appeared the hostess will announce: '*Kin Khao*' – eat rice – and the meal proper will begin.

That is our way of doing it but as the major hotels in Thailand have shown, it is no problem to separate off some of these appetizers, dips and salads as well as some of the smaller grilled dishes in order to make a first course. Soups and fish dishes can also make individual courses if required. It is up to the hosts – as long as the result is *Sanuk*, that's fine.

An everyday evening meal would normally be followed by fresh fruit. Thailand is famous for the high quality of its tropical fruits, and these would normally be peeled, sliced and neatly arranged on dishes before being offered to everyone; again that emphasis on sharing. If Thai sweets are served then ideally there should be two, one liquid, perhaps lotus seeds in coconut cream, and one dry, perhaps *Met Kanoon* made with egg, moong beans and sugar, and then fresh fruit last of all. After a full meal like that one's feelings should be *Sabai*, or well-being, the ultimate aim of all Thai activity.

In the heat of the kitchen

DRINKS

Iced tea brought to your boat – by boat!

The first-time visitor to a large Bangkok restaurant is always struck by the sight of diners arriving bearing bottles of whisky or brandy. A party out for the evening always takes its own drink, usually spirits, and this is then served, much iced and watered down, throughout the meal. This emphasis on spirits has reinforced the notion that Thai cuisine with its strong, hot flavours is not best accompanied by wine. To counter this, it is useful to know that the ancient Romans

Bangkok street vendor mixes fruit juice with crushed ice

flavoured their food with a liquid not unlike our fish sauce, that they were keen on strongly spiced dishes and yet drank wine with their meals. Of course, a delicate flavoured vintage would be somewhat wasted but any good robust wine goes well with anything other than the heavier curries. If you want to follow the Thai habit and stick with watered-down spirits, fair enough – there is even a Thai whisky 'Mekong', but it is not for the delicate! Other than that there is always lager and a Thai variety, 'Singha' is now sold abroad. For those who don't want alcohol suffice is to say that most Thais only drink water with their meals though a pleasant variant often found in Thailand is iced tea which is not only delicious but helps clear the palate.

ICED TEA

Cha Dam Yen

Dissolve sugar in boiling water to make a thin syrup. Make strong tea and allow to cool. Fill a tall glass with ice and add a slice of lemon, cover with tea and sweeten with syrup.

HOW TO USE THIS BOOK

Unless otherwise stated, all recipes are designed to make either:

A whole meal for one person
Part of a meal for two people with one other dish
Part of a meal for three people with three other dishes

In other words, portions are quite small, as it is the Thai custom to serve between three and five dishes at a meal, and if there are guests to add more dishes rather than just increase the amounts of what is already there.

In nearly all cases, cooking time is extremely short and it is therefore essential to have all your ingredients prepared and ready to hand before you begin.

MEASUREMENTS

I have not made any distinction between the UK and US measures of tablespoon and teaspoon – the differences are not vital to these recipes so long as the proportions are maintained by using the same spoon. They are always used as LEVEL measures. The metric equivalents of these measures are given as follows:

1 teaspoon (tsp)	=	5 ml
1 tablespoon (tbs)	=	15 ml

All equivalents have been rounded to the nearest convenient unit.

LIQUID MEASURES

1 US cup	=	8 fl oz	=	240 ml (approx. ¼ l)
1 US pint	=	16 fl oz	=	475 ml
1 UK pint	=	20 fl oz	=	570 ml

DRY MEASURES

You will find that I have used metric liquid measures (millilitres) for solid substances (eg. sugar, curry paste) where the amounts used are small, ie. teaspoons and tablespoons. It is much more simple to measure such amounts in this way rather than weigh them. There is no difference between UK and US weight measures; convenient metric equivalents are given as:

1 oz	=	30g
4 oz	=	120g
8 oz	=	230g
1 lb	=	450g

US cup dry measures can only be given imperial and metric equivalents for specific substances (to the nearest convenient unit):

1 cup flour	= 5oz	= 145g
1 cup granulated sugar	= 8oz	= 240g
1 cup dessicated coconut	= 2½oz	= 75g
1 cup peanuts	= 5oz	= 145g
1 cup sweetcorn (drained)	= 5½oz	= 165g
1 cup dry rice	= 7oz	= 210g
1 cup cooked rice	= 8oz	= 240g

Hand-sorting shallots in the sun

REFLECTIONS IN A
FIELD OF WATER

COUNTRY COOKING
FIRST STAGES & ELEMENTARY DISHES

in-khao, 'eat rice', the Thai way of summoning guests to a meal reveals how that simple white grain lies to the heart of our cuisine. When we eat we take rice first and use all other dishes as flavours to help demolish the little mountain on the plate before us. A true Thai feels unsettled if he doesn't eat rice at least once a day and no one doubts that the rice farmer is the most important worker in the kingdom. The paddy fields of the central plains, watered by a complex web of ancient irrigation channels are the real Thailand. Rice is our foremost export and the wealth it has brought has fostered succeeding civilizations and city states, from the now ruined Sukhothai down to present day Bangkok. Beyond that noisy sprawling metropolis another, timeless culture still survives. Speeding from city to city in a fast car you only glimpse this other world, across a flooded paddy field you see a cluster of wooden houses nestling beside the red and gold brilliance of a village temple, home to a way of life where modernity has a light touch. Buffaloes graze by the side of the super-highway, across a narrow bank raised above the water a woman staggers under the weight of two yoked panniers filled with fruit, after the city the air is sweet.

Only forty minutes drive from the centre of Bangkok you move straight back into that other world. Near the little market town of Hua Ta Keh the paddies stretch to the horizon broken only by the tiny hamlets on the banks of the *klongs* that flow into the Chao Phya. In May the rains come and everyone must go to the flooding fields for the arduous task of transplanting the little green shoots. In their shell-like straw hats the figures bend calf-deep in the glistening sea as if plucking at their own reflections in a vast mirror. Nothing that they do has altered since rice was first cultivated in the river basins of Asia; the jet aircraft screaming overhead could be a visitor from another planet.

Early photograph of a village stilt-house by a klong

Page 44: Raking over the rice harvest to dry out before it is sent down to Bangkok

*Steaming Thai
sweets in a
traditional kitchen
by a klong*

The dwellings here are not the stilt houses typical of much of Thailand. Here they live in low barn-like structures made of plaited bamboo-matting, the wide space covered with two pitched roofs. Here the farmer and all his family live with enough room for their buffalo. The farmer I visited recently no longer had an animal but shared the space with a rusting skeleton of a machine that he used for ploughing and which he called his 'mechanical buffalo'. His working day begins early and his wife starts to prepare food at five in the morning just before dawn. Instead of the traditional charcoal brazier she has an old metal stove that burns rice husks and a new electric rice-cooker, one of the few modern inventions of any use to her. For the rest, it is the usual display of metal pots and pans that you see stacked high in every market place. She cooks outside on a jetty washed by their *klong* from which her husband can dredge fish with a net on a frame not unlike a large broken umbrella. This is the most fertile part of the country and much of what they eat is freely to hand: many vegetables and herbs grow wild, others they cultivate on little plots near the house. In the busy planting season she often cooks only the most elementary Thai meal: boiled rice, a deep-fried fish served with her own version of the spicy *Nam Prik* sauce that is eaten everywhere in Thailand. When this simple meal is ready the family will not eat straight away, they are expecting a visitor and as the first light appears a long narrow boat is rowed into the *klong* by a monk in his vivid saffron robe. For the farmer and his wife this is the most important moment of their day, the placing of an offering of food in the alms bowl of their venerable visitor. It is a chance to uplift the spirit from the mundane tasks of the day by earning merit through giving.

With the coming of the rains and the rice safely planted,

*Village boys enter
their local
monastery during
the rainy season*

many of the young men of the village will become temporary
monks themselves. There will be an elaborate ceremony when
their heads are shaved and they are dressed in finery of white
fringed with gold, almost like brides, and are then carried
shoulder-high in procession to the temple. They will spend
three months purifying body and soul through prayer and
abstinence. The life of the farmer may be hard but it also has
great beauty. Few wish to change their lot as long as they can
provide food for their families. It is the impoverished people of
the dry north-east who leave the land for the dubious
advantages of the city. Perhaps with the city so near the
temptation is less. Just across the paddy is the King Mongkut
Institute of Technology where my brother teaches, it is home

Rice fields lead, after the harvest, to the village market. From there the crop finds its way to the great barges which are heading for Bangkok

to the biggest computer centre in the country, yet the farmer still uses an ancient machine like a wooden treadmill in a long box, to raise water from the *klong* to the ditches that irrigate his fields. His only connection with the capital comes when he and his wife rest during the afternoon heat and listen to the transistor radio that brings the latest gripping instalment of the current soap opera – a village girl has been taken up by a city slicker. She is beautiful, he is persuasive and has convinced her to leave her family and her village to go with him to Bangkok. What will happen to her there? Are his intentions honourable? All over the country millions of people are listening to the same story. In the farmer's house it is the cause of much head-shaking.

Pinned to a post in the house is an old calendar, kept because it bears a photograph of King Bhumiphol whose image is venerated. To the farmer the king is part of the mystical process that ensures a good harvest. In May at the beginning of the rainy season, the king presides over the ancient ploughing ceremony on the Pramane Ground outside the walls of the Grand Palace in Bangkok. This is a Brahmin ceremony; Buddhism in Thailand embraces much of Hinduism and our early sovereigns kept Brahmin priests and astrologers as permanent members of their court. At the ceremony the Brahmins begin by offering special delicacies to placate the Gods and then two sacred oxen, covered in cloth of gold, are led forward by attendants in bright red costumes. The oxen drag a ceremonial plough, the priests sprinkle Holy water and women scatter rice from gold and silver vessels. Drawn up before the king the beasts are offered their choice of grains, beans or liquor to indicate whether the coming harvest will be good or bad – if they choose the liquor it is a disaster! Once the king has left, the waiting crowd dashes onto the field in a mad scrabble to retrieve the 'lucky' rice. Many young people travel long distances from their villages hoping to return with a few grains believing that if planted in their fields a good yield will be assured.

For our farmer, the only place outside his hamlet that concerns him is the market town of Hua Ta Keh. In November the rice is winnowed in a huge woven basket and any surplus is taken by boat down to where the klong widens into the town. Wooden shop houses are stretched along both banks and here all local commerce takes place. Traditionally the rice merchants have been Chinese, though intermarriage has made most indistinguishable from the rest of the population. Their shops have a dark nineteenth-century air, with wood and glass cabinets, leather-bound ledgers and prints that show the rotund jovial man who sold for cash set against his thin, unhappy rival who foolishly sold on credit. Nestling under the steep wooden bridge that links the two banks is one of the most famous sights in Thailand, a floating market of narrow boats that have brought the produce of the farms: fruit and vegetables, craftwork and prepared delicacies. It is a sight full of colour and with the money they have earned the farmer and his wife can buy the few modern things they need: batteries and plastic mugs, the spices they do not grow on their farm and perhaps indulge themselves with delicious Thai sweetmeats sizzling on hot griddles.

In the town there is a Chinese temple, not dedicated to a god but to a local businessman who, having made his fortune and provided for his family as every good Chinese should, gave up the cares of this life through prayer and fasting. His gilded emaciated statue squats in a niche at the end of the prayer hall, lit by candles and wafted with incense. It is businesses such as his that send the rice down the *klong* to be transferred onto enormous, hangar-like rice barges that will carry it down the Chao Phya to the warehouses at Klong Tuey, the capital's harbour, and thus to the cargo vessels that will transport it world-wide. I would doubt the farmer knows much of all that – he works, his family eats well, that is enough. Their lives are punctuated with temple festivals and other celebrations. At the end of the rains, when the harvest is in and the moon is full there is *Loy Krathong*, the time to give thanks to the Mother of Rivers. A *krathong*, a small dish-shaped raft, is made out of bamboo leaves and decorated with flowers. Onto this is put a lit candle and incense. *Loy* means to float and the little rafts are lowered into the water to be born away. If your candle continues to flicker as it floats away from you it will carry with it all the misfortunes of the past year. The farmer and his family can watch their delicate craft until it is lost round a curve in the *klong* that will lead on into the Chao Phya. Who knows, it may carry on downstream to the fabled gilded towers and temples of the City of Angels itself.

The heart of Thai cooking

RICE
Khao Suay

Using the recipes in this chapter, you can start with one or two individual dishes but quickly work up to a full meal. The first essential is good rice. A Thai cook will know from experience whether rice is young or old; young rice needs to be cooked in less water than old, as it still contains some natural moisture. In Thailand we use what we call 'fragrant' rice, a good quality long-grain rice. But it is probable that all rice available in Europe and North America is 'old', and therefore completely dry, and will need slightly more water to cook in.

As I have already said, an electric rice-cooker is a wise investment for regular rice eaters, otherwise a little technique is needed to get your rice light and fluffy, with each grain separate. Succeed in this and you have got your Thai meal off to a flying start.

1 lb/450g rice
1pt/500ml water

Rinse the rice thoroughly at least three times in cold water until the water runs clear. Put the rice in a heavy saucepan and add the water. Cover and quickly bring to the boil. Uncover, and while it is cooking stir vigorously until all the water has evaporated. Turn the heat down as low as possible, re-cover (put a layer of foil under the lid if necessary to make sure of a tight fit) and steam for 20 minutes.

FRIED CHICKEN WITH BAMBOO SHOOTS ON RICE
Khao Nah Gai

This dish is a meal in itself, served *on* rice rather than as one of several dishes making up a full meal. Most of its ingredients can be found in cans so it makes a useful emergency meal.

1 lb/450g/2cups cooked rice
2 tbs/30ml oil
2 garlic cloves, finely chopped
4oz/120g boneless chicken, finely sliced
2oz/60g bamboo shoots, sliced
2oz/60g straw mushrooms, halved
1 tbs/15ml light soy sauce
2 tbs/30ml fish sauce
1 tsp/5ml sugar
1 tbs/15ml dark soy sauce
3 tbs/45ml stock/broth or water (or more if necessary)
1 tbs/15ml flour mixed with 2 tbs/30ml water (this is probably more than you will need)
a shaking of ground white pepper
1 spring onion/scallion, coarsely chopped

Put the cooked rice on a serving dish and keep warm. In a wok or frying pan heat the oil until a light haze appears. Add the garlic and cook until golden brown. Add the chicken and stir-fry for a few seconds. Add the bamboo shoots and straw mushrooms and stir. Stirring quickly after each addition, add the light soy, fish sauce, sugar, dark soy and stock (or water). Add more stock if the mixture becomes dry. Add 1 tbs/15ml of the flour and water mixture and stir until thoroughly blended to make a lightly thickened sauce, adding a little more stock or flour/water mixture if necessary. Add the pepper and chopped spring onions, stir quickly and serve immediately over the cooked rice.

Opposite: Moo Pad King, *Pork fried with ginger, and* Gung Kratiem, *Prawns with garlic quick to prepare with easily available ingredients*

PRAWNS WITH GARLIC
Gung Kratiem

lettuce, parsley sprigs and cucumber slices, to garnish
2 tbs/30ml oil
2 large garlic cloves, finely chopped
6-9 large raw king prawns, shelled and deveined
1 tbs/15ml fish sauce
1 tbs/15ml light soy sauce
1 tbs/15ml dark soy sauce
4 tbs/60ml stock/broth or water
a shaking of ground white pepper

Line a serving dish with lettuce, parsley sprigs and a few slices of cucumber. Reserve.

In a wok or frying pan, heat the oil until a light haze appears. Add the garlic and fry until golden brown. Add the prawns and cook briefly, stirring all the time, until they start to become opaque. Stirring briskly after each addition, add the fish sauce, light soy, dark soy, stock and white pepper. By now the prawns should be cooked through. Turn the heat up to maximum for a few seconds quickly to reduce the liquid to about 3 tbs/45ml. Turn onto the prepared serving dish and serve.

FRIED VEGETABLES WITH PORK
Moo Pad Pak

This, and the next four recipes, would make central dishes for a balanced Thai meal – I'll give two sample 'menus' towards the end of the chapter. This first dish is only mildly flavoured and depends for its quality on the al dente firmness of the vegetables.

4oz/120g lean pork, finely diced
1 tbs/15ml fish sauce
grinding of black pepper
2 tbs/30ml oil
1 garlic clove, finely chopped
1 lb/450g prepared raw vegetables (any combination of mangetout/snow peas, cauliflower and broccoli trimmed into small florets, sliced courgettes/zucchini)
3 tbs/45ml fish sauce
2 tbs/30ml light soy sauce
½ tsp/2-3ml sugar
¼pt/120ml water, as necessary

Put the first three ingredients in a small bowl, mix thoroughly and set aside.

In a wok or frying pan, heat the oil until a light haze appears. Add the garlic and fry until golden brown. Add the pork mixture and stir-fry briefly until the meat is opaque. Add the prepared vegetables and stir. Add the fish sauce, soy sauce, sugar, a grinding of black pepper and a little water. Stirring constantly, and adding a little more water if the mixture is becoming too dry (you should have about ¼pt/120ml total liquid), continue to stir until the mangetout are bright green and the other vegetables are still crisp. This should take no more than 3-4 minutes – less is best, as the vegetables must not be overcooked and must retain their crispness.

PORK FRIED WITH GINGER
Moo Pad King

This recipe can be also made equally success-fully with chicken or beef.

3 tbs/45ml oil
2 garlic cloves, finely chopped
4oz/120g boneless pork, finely sliced
6 pieces dried mushroom, soaked in water for 10 minutes to soften and then coarsely chopped
2in/5cm piece ginger, peeled and finely slivered
1 tbs/15ml light soy sauce
1 tbs/15ml dark soy sauce
¼ tsp/1-2ml sugar
2 tbs/30ml stock/broth or water
1 tbs/15ml fish sauce
½ small onion, slivered
1 long red chilli, trimmed and cut into slivers (deseed if you wish to reduce the heat)
1 spring onion/scallion, green part only, cut into 1in/2½cm long pieces
ground white pepper

In a wok or frying pan, heat the oil until a light haze appears. Add the garlic and fry until golden brown. Add the pork, stir and cook for a minute or two until the meat is opaque. Add the mushrooms and ginger and stir thorough-ly. Stirring briskly after each addition, add the soy sauces, sugar, stock or water, fish sauce, onion and chilli. Cook for a few seconds more, transfer to a serving dish, garnish with the spring onion pieces and sprinkle lightly with ground white pepper.

CHICKEN FRIED WITH CHILLI AND NUTS
Gai Pad Prik Haeng

This and the next recipe are chilli hot, but you can reduce the heat by removing the seeds from the chillies before cooking. The pleasure of this dish is the contrast between the soft meat and the crunchy nuts.

2 tbs/30ml oil
1 garlic clove, finely chopped
5-6 dried long chillies, with or without seeds, chopped
4 oz/120g chicken breast, finely sliced
1 tbs/15 ml fish sauce
1 heaped tbs/20g roasted peanuts
6-8 small thin French/snap beans, cut in 1in/2½cm pieces
3 tbs/45ml stock/broth
1 tbs/15ml light soy sauce
1 tbs/15ml dark soy sauce
¼ tsp/1-2ml sugar

In a wok or frying pan heat the oil until a light haze appears. Fry the garlic until golden brown. Add the chillies and stir. Add the chicken meat, stir and cook until the meat is slightly opaque. Stirring after each addition, add the remaining ingredients, one by one. Cook for a minute or two, making sure the meat is cooked through, and serve.

CHICKEN WITH CURRY POWDER
Gai Pad Pung Kari

We like to include at least one curry in a full meal and in the next chapter I'll show how to make up the different pastes that are the basis of the four main curries. However, before we start the business of pounding spices, we have easier dishes like this which use ready-made curry powder – a medium Indian curry powder will do.

2 tbs/30ml oil
2 garlic cloves, finely chopped
1 tbs/15ml curry powder
4 oz/120g chicken breast, coarsely chopped
1 small onion, chopped
1 medium potato, diced small
about 8 tbs/120ml stock/broth or water
2 tbs/30ml fish sauce
pinch of sugar
4 tbs/60ml coconut milk

In a wok or frying pan, heat the oil until a light haze appears. Add the garlic and fry until golden brown. Add the curry powder, stir to mix thoroughly and cook for 1 minute. Add the chicken, stir and mix until the meat is coated with the curry mixture. Add the onion, potato and 4 tbs/60ml stock, and cook, stirring constantly until the potato is *al dente*. If the mixture becomes dry, add a little more stock. Add the fish sauce, sugar and coconut milk, stirring after each addition. Cook until the liquid is slightly thickened.

BEAN CURD SOUP
Gaeng Jued Tao Hou

Everything about a Thai meal aims at a balance of flavours, and to offset the chilli level in the last two dishes you should give each diner a small bowl of lightly-flavoured clear soup which can be sipped to relax the palate.

1pt/500ml chicken stock/broth
2 tbs/30ml fish sauce
1 tbs/15ml light soy sauce
1 tsp/5ml preserved radish (*tang chi*, p.39)
½ tsp/2ml ground white pepper
4oz/120g bean curd, cut into 16 × ½in/1cm cubes
2 spring onions/scallions, green part only, cut in 1in/2½cm slivers
Serves up to 4

In a medium saucepan, heat together the chicken stock, fish sauce, soy sauce, preserved radish and white pepper. When simmering, add the cubes of bean curd, cook for half a minute and then add the pieces of spring onion. Simmer for a few seconds, ladle into small bowls and serve.

Traditional Thai brooms

VERMICELLI SOUP
Gaeng Jued Wun Sen

2 tbs oil

2 garlic cloves, finely chopped

1pt/500ml chicken stock/broth

1 tsp/5ml preserved radish (*tang chi*, p. 39)

4oz/120g minced/ground pork, roughly shaped into 10-12 small balls

2oz/60g, dry weight, clear vermicelli (*Wun Sen*, p. 86) soaked for 10 minutes in cold water to soften, and drained

1 tbs/15ml fish sauce

1 tbs/15ml light soy sauce

¼ tsp/1-2ml sugar

4-5 pieces of dried mushroom, soaked for 10 minutes in cold water to soften, drained and coarsely chopped

1 small onion, finely chopped

½ tsp/2ml ground white pepper

1 spring onion/scallion, green part only, slivered lengthways

In a small frying pan, heat the oil until a light haze appears. Add the garlic and fry until golden brown. Set aside.

In a medium saucepan, quickly heat the stock with the preserved radish. When the liquid is simmering, add the balls of minced pork and cook for a few seconds. Add the drained noodles and stir thoroughly. Add the fish sauce, soy sauce, sugar, mushrooms, onion and white pepper, stirring thoroughly after each addition. By this time the meat should be quite cooked through. Remove from heat and pour into bowl. Pour a little of the fried garlic and oil into each bowl and garnish with the spring onion.

DEEP-FRIED SPARE-RIBS
Grat Dook Moo Tod

As well as the substantial 'main' dishes and the balancing soups, an ideal meal should also offer at least one tasty side dish. This one, and the next three recipes, all have very distinctive flavours. Spare-ribs are, of course, now part of 'international' cuisine, but these are happily

Previous pages: A complete Thai meal: Gai Pad Prik Haeng, *Chicken fried with chilli and nuts;* Grat Dook Moo Tod, *deep-fried spare-ribs;* Prik Pak Dong, *Pickled cabbage;* Gaeng Jued Tao Hou, *Bean curd soup;* Kai Look Koei, *Son-in-law eggs – and, of course, rice*

Thai woven textile

quite different from the usual barbecue-sauce offerings found elsewhere.

4 garlic cloves, finely chopped

4 large coriander roots, chopped

2 tbs/30ml flour

1 egg

2 tbs/30ml fish sauce

2 tbs/30ml light soy sauce

1 lb/450g pork spare-ribs, chopped into 1½-2in/4-5cm pieces (ask your butcher to do this for you)

oil for deep frying

Using a pestle and mortar or a blender, pound or blend the garlic and coriander roots together. In a large bowl, mix the flour with the egg, fish sauce and soy sauce, and add the garlic and coriander mixture. Mix thoroughly. Add the pork rib pieces and turn them until each piece is covered with the mixture. Leave for at least half an hour.

Heat the oil in a deep-fryer until a light haze appears. Fry the pieces of rib for about 6-8 minutes until well-browned. Remove with a slotted spoon, drain and serve.

FRIED MARINATED BEEF
Nua Cheh Nam Pla

2 tbs/30ml fish sauce
1 tsp/5ml salt
1 tsp/5ml sugar
1 tbs/15ml oil, plus 6 tbs/90 ml oil for frying
1 lb/450g skirt or flank beef, sliced diagonally across the grain into about 8-10 pieces

In a medium bowl mix the fish sauce, salt, sugar and 1 tbs/15ml oil. Add the pieces of beef and turn them thoroughly in the mixture. Leave to marinate for at least an hour. Remove the meat and drain on a rack. In Thailand, after marinating we would put the meat in the sun to dry: this can be simulated simply by leaving it overnight. If you wish to eat straight away, put the pieces of meat under a low grill or in a warm oven for about 10-15 minutes until dry. To finish, heat the oil in a frying pan until a very light haze appears and fry the meat on both sides until it is dark brown – about 5 minutes.

STEAMED EGG
Kai Toon

If you don't have a steamer, use a large lidded pan instead. Upturn a bowl in the bottom of the pan, add water to come about half-way up the upturned bowl and place the dish of eggs on top. Cover the pan and steam. Make sure the pan is large enough for you to remove the dish of cooked eggs easily.

3 large eggs
2oz/60g minced/ground pork
1 spring onion/scallion, trimmed and finely chopped
1 shallot, finely chopped
3 tbs/45ml fish sauce
1 tsp/5ml ground white pepper
1 tbs/15ml water
1 tsp/5ml finely chopped coriander leaf

Break the eggs into a deep bowl which can be easily removed from your steamer or pan. Add the pork, chopped spring onion and shallot, fish sauce, white pepper and water. Lightly beat together. Add the chopped coriander and stir. Place the bowl in the steamer or pan and steam for 12-15 minutes until the egg is set – test it with the tines of a fork; they should come out clean with no liquid on them.

Traditionally patterned material

SON-IN-LAW EGGS
Kai Look Koei

This dish is famous in Thailand as much for its name as its taste. 'Eggs', needless to say, is a euphemism!

6 eggs
oil for deep-frying, plus 2 tbs/30ml
1 small onion, finely sliced
4 tbs/60ml fish sauce
2 tbs/30ml sugar
½ tsp/2-3ml crushed dried chilli or chilli powder

Hard-boil/cook the eggs for 6-8 minutes. Rinse in cold water and shell. Heat the oil in the deep-fryer or wok until a light haze appears. Using a slotted spoon, lower the eggs into the oil and fry gently, turning carefully, until they are a light golden brown. Remove from the oil, drain, halve lengthways and arrange on a serving dish. Set aside.

In a small frying pan, heat the remaining oil until a light haze appears. Fry the sliced onion until crisp and deep brown. Remove from the pan with a slotted spoon, drain and set aside. There should be a film of oil left in the pan. Turn the heat down low and add the fish sauce, sugar and chilli. Cook slowly, stirring, until the sugar has dissolved. Continue to cook for about a minute until the mixture thickens, then add the reserved onions and stir for a few seconds to mix. Remove immediately from the heat, pour over the eggs and serve.

PICKLED CABBAGE
Prik Pak Dong

This pickle is easy to make and goes well with simple dishes. The 'pickling' is achieved by the action of the garlic, sugar and salt on the cabbage, forming a liquid. It will keep in an airtight jar in the refrigerator for 2-3 weeks, but no longer.

1 Chinese cabbage (Chinese leaves), about 2lbs/1kg
3 garlic cloves, finely chopped
2 large red chillies, finely chopped
1 tbs/15ml sugar
2 tbs/30ml salt

Cut the leafy top (about 1½-2in/4-5cm) from the cabbage and use it in another dish, or as a salad.

Trim away the base of the cabbage and cut the remainder into 2 in/5cm slices. Put into a large bowl, add the remaining ingredients and mix thoroughly. Spoon into a preserving or similar jar, seal the jar and leave for 3 days in a cool place (larder, pantry or refrigerator).

You now have enough recipes to create a full meal. Here are two suggested menus which you can shuffle around as you wish and which will adequately feed 3-4 people:

A
Rice
Chicken fried with chilli and nuts
Bean curd soup
Deep-fried spare-ribs
Son-in-law eggs
Pickled cabbage

B
Rice
Pork fried with ginger
Vermicelli soup
Fried marinated beef
Steamed egg

FRIED RICE WITH CHICKEN AND CURRY POWDER
Khao Pad Karee Gai

Separate from full meal dishes are those 'mopping-up' recipes that can provide lunch or a quick snack. Fried rice is the classic 'day-after' method of using up the extra rice from the night before. It is always a separate meal in Thailand; it would be rather eccentric to serve it in place of plain boiled rice as the staple for a dinner.

I suggest three recipes here but you can make up your own variations when you've mastered the technique. In all fried rice dishes, use less rather than more oil. The result should be dry, with the rice grains separate.

At a Bangkok rice warehouse

2 tbs/30ml oil
2 garlic cloves, finely chopped
2 tsp/10 ml medium-hot curry powder
3oz/90g boneless chicken, chopped or finely sliced
1 lb/450g/2½ cups cooked rice
1 tbs/15ml light soy sauce
2 tbs/15ml fish sauce
¼ tsp/1-2 ml sugar
1 spring onion/scallion, trimmed, and slivered into 1in/2½cm lengths
½ small onion, finely slivered
a shaking of ground white pepper

In a wok or frying pan, heat the oil until a light haze appears. Add the garlic and fry until golden brown. Add the curry powder, stir and cook for a few seconds; add the chicken and cook for a minute or two until the meat is opaque. Add the rice and stir thoroughly. Add the soy sauce, fish sauce and sugar, stirring after each addition. Cook together for a few seconds until you are certain that the meat is cooked and the rice thoroughly reheated. Turn onto serving dish, garnish with the spring onion, and onion, and lightly sprinkle with pepper.

PINEAPPLE-FRIED RICE

Khao Pad Supparot

I have included this as much for the chance it offers for a theatrical presentation as for any other reason. Using the whole, fresh pineapple as the serving dish looks marvellous and is really very easy. It is important to choose the pineapple carefully: it should be ripe, sweet and juicy.

1 pineapple
3 shallots, coarsely chopped
1 large red chilli, finely slivered
1 spring onion/scallion, green part only, coarsely chopped
1 sprig of coriander, coarsely chopped
2 tbs/30ml oil
2 tbs/30ml dried shrimp
2 garlic cloves, finely chopped
1 lb/450g/2cups cooked rice
1 tbs/15ml fish sauce
1 tbs/15ml light soy sauce
1 tsp/5ml sugar
coriander leaves, to garnish

Cut the pineapple in half lengthways. If the fruit is large, set one half aside to eat as dessert. Hollow the flesh out of both halves, chopping it into ½ in/1cm cubes. Put the pineapple flesh in a bowl, and add the shallots, chilli, scallion and coriander; mix and set aside.

In a wok or frying pan/skillet, heat 1 tbs/15ml oil, add the dried shrimp and fry until crispy. With a slotted spoon, remove the shrimp, drain and set aside. Add the remaining 1 tbs/15ml oil, heat, add the garlic and fry until golden brown. Add the cooked rice, stir thoroughly. Add the fish sauce, soy sauce and sugar. Stir and mix thoroughly. Make sure the rice is heated through, then add the pineapple mixture and the crispy shrimp. Mix all thoroughly and heat through. Fill the pineapple shell(s) with the mixture, garnish with a little more coriander and serve.

FRIED RICE WITH PRAWN AND CHILLIES

Khao Pad Prik Gung

2 tbs/30ml oil
2 garlic cloves, finely chopped
2 small red chillies, finely chopped
4oz/120g peeled prawns
1 tbs/15ml fish sauce
¼ tsp/1-2ml sugar
1 tbs/15ml light soy sauce
1 lb/450g/2½ cups cooked rice
½ small onion, slivered
½ red or green sweet pepper, slivered
½ tsp/2.5ml ground white pepper
1 spring onion/scallion, green part only, slivered into 1in/2½ cm lengths
coriander leaves, to garnish

In a wok or frying pan, heat the oil until a light haze appears. Add the garlic and fry until golden brown. Add the chillies and the prawns and stir quickly. Add the fish sauce, sugar and soy sauce; stir and cook for a few seconds until the prawns are cooked through. Add the cooked rice and stir thoroughly. Add the onion, sweet pepper, white pepper and spring onion and stir quickly to mix. Turn onto a serving dish and garnish with the coriander leaves.

CITY OF ANGELS

BANGKOK LIFE
MORE ADVANCED FOOD

1 n the darkness three linked rice barges plough down the Chao Phya, low in the water. A light flickers at the stern of the forward vessel – the cooking fire of the family for whom this is a permanent home. They pass through the centre of old Bangkok, past rickety wooden houses built out into the river on stilts, past the green-tiled roofs and golden spires of the Grand Palace, and the Temple of the Emerald Buddha, Thailand's national shrine. On the opposite bank, in Thonburi, the tallest spire of all, Wat Arun, the Temple of the Dawn, appropriately catches the first light which plays on the vivid shards of Chinese pottery used to make its dazzling mosaic shell. King Taksin, the Chinese General who saved the Thai nation after our defeat by the Burmese in the eighteenth century, set up his headquarters in Thonburi while he drove the invaders from our land. It was his successor King Rama I who moved the capital to its present site and gave it the name we use – Krung Thep, the City of Angels. Early foreign visitors used the name of the nearby port – Bangkok, 'place of the wild

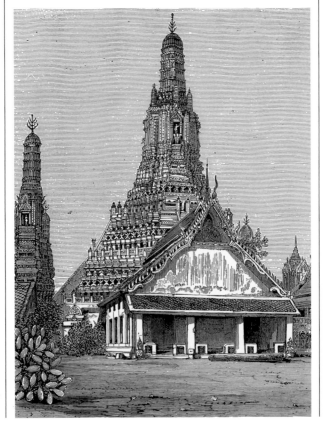

Early engraving of The Temple of the Dawn

*Previous pages:
The Temple of the Dawn
seen across the Chao
Phya river*

Restoring the Grand Palace for the bicentennial of Bangkok in 1986

plum', and that has remained in languages other than ours. Originally, the city was waterborne, with dwellings built on rafts and even after more permanent houses were built, Krung Thep was for much of its history a place of canals and streams with most movement by boat. Today, the last symbol of that era is the rarely-held Royal Barge Procession when the King and Queen cross the river in ornately carved galleys to offer new robes to the monks at Wat Arun, the scarlet-coated rowers slashing the water in unison, kept in time by a rhythm-keeper tapping the butt of his silver spear on the deck. Even without such ceremony, the river bank still deludes the early morning visitor into thinking that little has changed: naked children dive into the murky waters both to clean themselves and just for the fun of it, the flat-bottomed boats arrive from the countryside at the market jetties to unload their produce, a ferry crosses the river carrying a group of young monks from upcountry come to study at one of the city's great monastic schools. But pass through the Ba Klong Dalat market to Chakapetch Road and the past begins to recede. Noisy *tuctucs*, a sort of motorized rickshaw, sputter and snarl, loaded with fruit and vegetables for the smaller local markets and for the city's innumerable restaurants. Further down the road is the flower market with enormous cascades of mauve orchids or violent tubs of blood-red roses; flowers in the tropics are never restrained and here their abundance astonishes. Among the shops along the pavement where the flower-sellers congregate are the main tea dealers. Early in the morning Mr Liew Hua Choon opens his business and reveals a charming glimpse of turn of the century Bangkok – an interior made up of shelves of laquered canisters with gold Thai lettering and a wall of painted-glass cabinets in glowing colours. His assistants deftly weigh out small portions of scented tea, then use a sort of origami to turn the flat wrapping paper into a neat box with the label always uppermost. There are beautifully decorated tins of tea in graded qualities, the finest having a subtle hint of jasmin. Walk in and you will be offered a tasting from the brown metal teapot warming at the back of the shop.

Outside, on the pavement, the flower-sellers breakfast in the pauses between customers, holding bowls of rice porridge which they spoon up with slivers of red roasted pork and nibbles of salty preserved vegetables. The porters stop from their frantic dashing about to buy a helping of *Tow Hoo Tod*; golden-brown beancurd that sizzles in a deep fryer at one of the stalls. A day of street food has begun.

At the other side of town, near my family home, where the two broad highways, Silom Road and Rama IV Road intersect, the towers are no longer elegant gilded spires but soaring concrete skyscrapers topped with the aerials and radar dishes that link the capital's business district into the world's telecommunications network. We have exchanged an oriental Venice for an eastern Los Angeles where the rising sun is reflected in the vast mirror wall of a bank's headquarters. Soon every broad road and narrow *soi* will be blocked with the choking rush-hour traffic. But in the last moments before the work day begins you can walk into Lumpini Park, one of the rare green spaces in the city, and see sights few tourists ever witness. Just inside the main gates, beyond the statue of King Rama VI, is a crowd of at least a hundred middle-aged people, the ladies wearing black trousers and simple cotton blouses, all wriggling away to disco music from a ghetto-blaster. They are very straight-faced and are concentrating hard on what they are doing. This is no pleasure outing, this is health. A little further away on one of the lawns a man in shorts and tee-shirt is barking orders at a horde of elderly men and women who stretch and bend in unison, following the prescribed gestures of Tai Chi, the ancient Chinese system of exercise that looks not unlike Kung Fu in slow motion. A posse of young Thai students in Adidas sweat-shirts and Reebok trainers sweats it round the circuitous paths that link the wooden fretwork pavilions and ornamental pagodas. They are getting in practice for the city's marathon. Many of the elderly have come from the far suburbs, travelling during the small hours just to enjoy a little company in the open air before the city is taken over by the pushing throng of clerks and shop assistants. With a bulging population of eight million in a place that was until recently a sleepy town criss-crossed with canals, there are precious few interludes like this. Near to one of the side entrances a breakfast market has grown up on the site of what used to be an open-air restaurant. Here, under canvas awnings you can find the whole range of Bangkok food, though the emphasis is still on health, with lots of vegetarian dishes and rice porridge made with 'red' rice. My own favourite breakfast in the park is a hot soup of beancurd that has been boiled with ginger, almost a sweet course really, but very refreshing. After the hot taste of ginger you can breathe clearly.

Near the entrance one smart entrepreneur has put down a

Opposite: Bangkok taxis, called tuctucs. The Vespa and the rickshaw have been combined into a noisome three-wheeler

Top: The author's mother making an offering to her family's Spirit House. Right: Thai fast food. Chicken with rice

set of bathroom scales and is charging one *baht* a go. A plump matron who has danced for an hour then eaten for almost as long pays to see what effect this has had on her waistline. There are monks waiting near the gate to receive offerings. Some people buy food in the market to place in their alms bowls while others offer bank notes. Thus, with exercise and charity both body and soul are refreshed.

A short walk away, at my parents' house, religion also figures at the start of the day. Before her children and grandchildren begin the scramble for breakfast, my mother sets out an offering of tea in a fine china cup on a lacquer tray and takes it to the highest room in the building, which houses

Old and new Bangkok compete. The Golden Mount on the right confronts the skyscraper blocks that house international banks

our family shrine. She sets the offering before the statue of the Buddha, lights a stick of incense and says a silent prayer. Some days my mother also takes offerings of food to the spirit house, a model Thai dwelling standing on a pillar in the garden. This is a home for *Pra Poom*, the spirit of the land who was displaced when our house was built. Failure to placate him, or to seek his blessing when there are difficulties, or when someone returns home after a voyage, may lead to all sorts of trouble. Visitors, particularly from the West are always intrigued by our animist beliefs – 'Do you really believe that?' is their usual cry. I suppose the answer is that we look on this as a case of better safe than sorry. When the Erewan Hotel was being built several

Boat-noodles by a klong

of the workers were mysteriously injured before the management erected a large shrine to the Hindu god *Shiva* and the problems ended. Today the Erewan shrine is a major gathering point where supplicants come to get luck in the National Lottery or to ask for good fortune in some coming enterprise. If you are lucky you must go back and offer garlands of jasmin, candles and incense and even pay for a performance of Thai classical dancing to please the deity. The bigger the building, the bigger the spirit house: there are huge spirit houses outside skyscraper banks, and even a model 'spirit mountain' on the road to Hua Hin where the real mountain is being mined. Whenever there is a special reason for gratitude, my mother will offer *Pra Poom* a feast: a boiled pig's head, a boiled chicken, a large steamed fish, boiled rice, the seasonal fruits, a selection of sweetmeats and a drink. A table is set up in front of the spirit house, always before ten in the morning, and this is decorated with vases of water lilies and yellow candles. Fortunately, after about an hour, when he is thought to be satisfied we can take back the food and enjoy it ourselves. I was always intrigued by the fact that the legions of ants and other insects in our garden never touched this succulent fare, until a friend with a more rational mind pointed out that it was probably the smoking joss-sticks that kept them away.

Breakfast in our house is a case of grab what you want before dashing off to work, or while getting the children ready for the school bus. No different from anywhere. Sometimes a Thai breakfast of rice soup with minced pork and preserved radish is boiled up with the left-over rice from the night before. But more often it is ham, eggs and toast. American food has now been absorbed into our cuisine and dotted around Bangkok are branches of most of the major international fast food chains – such as McDonald's, Dunkin' Donut, and Wimpy – and happily these are treated more like exotic oddities than as serious substitutes for our own diet, probably because

Pages 72/73: The Royal Barge Procession

Thailand is already the home of fast food. Almost every street corner in the city boasts a cluster of stalls with little stools selling everything from a tiny savoury appetizer to a full dish of rice and meat. Some thoroughfares off the main streets are effectively open-air restaurants and there are unnumbered cooks who rise early everyday to prepare their stock before heading off for their spot on the pavement. Each one specializes: there's the man who is up before dawn preparing the beef balls that he will slot onto skewers, grill and serve with little plastic bags of sweet sauce; there's the woman who will sit cross-legged all day spreading batter onto a charcoal-heated griddle making pancakes. Some of these stalls are elaborate portable kitchens with metal and glass cabinets that display neat patterns of vegetables, shiny brown duck, snowy coils of river noodles. In the residential areas, the travelling cooks used to plod down the quiet *sois* calling out their wares. They always seemed to have worked out how to pass in the right order so that the housewife who didn't want to cook could begin with an appetizer, wait and then find that the noodle-seller was passing, eat, and then see that the seller of desserts was coming her way. Today, there's more likely to be a small food market where the *soi* joins the main road – a short walk but still very convenient. More than any, it is the noodle-sellers who seem to be everywhere. If you are by a river, they turn up on boats, the steaming boiler borne along on the low-bottomed craft. There is a noodle vendor near every garage in the remotest countryside, and I doubt anyone could estimate the number in the capital. They are the city workers' best friends, providing a cheap, quick lunch instantly, and it is always a pleasure to watch the usually buxom cook rapidly turning the noodles in her wok, tossing in the spicy ingredients at high speed. You can almost hear the murmur of pleasure rising over Bangkok at lunchtime.

My aunt is a senior official in the Bangkok Bank, and on the top floor of their high modern headquarters the chief executives can lunch at a buffet of the best Thai cooking – but do not weep for the humbler clerks for they can eat as well, if not better, in the teeming market in the streets below. We are lucky, in that fine cuisine in our country is not the prerogative of the rich, and my aunt finds it no hardship to skip the grand food from time to time and to slip out to her favourite noodle restaurant.

Noodles are of course Chinese in origin, and the Chinese business community were some of the original residents of the area. When the new capital was being built they were moved further down river to make way for the Grand Palace, and Sampeng, the resettled area, is now one of the city's oldest quarters. But the main bustling Chinatown is Yowarat, a maze of narrow streets with the many famous bullion shops, bright red and gold emporia, glittering with mirrors in which are reflected the gold chains that are sold by weight and length. Chinatown too has its countless restaurants, and if it is hard to imagine the number of noodle-sellers in the city, it is even harder to imagine how many ducks are sold in Yowarat. I love to look inside the wooden stores with their lacquered boxes and bulbous jars of snake wine and other strange medicines, or the rice merchant with his hessian sacks and heavy Victorian scales. When you look there is always somebody with his head in a bowl and his chopsticks clicking away. The best thing in Chinatown is a visit to one of the many astrologers sitting at a table in one of the Chinese shrines to have him cast your horoscope. I like to watch the patient artistry with which he writes out my future in elegant Chinese characters.

Near to Chinatown is the Indian Market which sells mostly fabrics. India is the other side of the coin that makes up our food and in contrast to the lightness of Chinese noodles stand the rich curries that we have taken into our cuisine. We use the same ingredients as the Indian curries: turmeric, cumin, star

Last meal of the day, a bowl of noodles by the road-side

anise, coriander, but adapted in our own way. We like to have at least one curry with a full meal, and my own favourite is my mother's green curry, always made for me the night when I arrive home.

So it is the evening meal. The tourists who have been working hard, visiting the reclining Buddha or climbing to the top of the Golden Mount, or swaying by coach to the ruins of Ayuthaya are probably doing one last walk down the lines of heated chafing dishes for their buffet supper. Thai food has proved remarkably adaptable to this sort of mass catering, especially the curries which don't have to be quick-fried at the last moment. No doubt these visitors have remarked on the number of outside food stalls there are but may have felt too nervous to try them. A recent solution is Silom Village at the centre of the hotel district, which has a series of wooden Thai houses linked by a winding lane where there are clusters of food stalls. The visitor can see just what it is they are going to get, and can try this new ex- perience with more confidence. This isn't just another tourist trap because at lunchtime you'll find plenty of Thais en- joying a meal there. At our home, mother organizes the evening meal with the help of her daughter and daughters-in- law – we all eat together. While the smallest children are given their supper, my father has his whisky and nibbles on some tidbits bought by my brothers on their way home from work – some *Tod Man*, chewy fishcake with a dip of cucumber and crushed peanuts, perhaps. My mother calls out *Kin Khao* and the rice is ladled out. The young girl who acts as nursemaid to the children crouches by the television glued to the latest soap – a girl from the countryside has met a rich man from the city, etc., etc. . . .

The author selecting vegetables

For the tired workers this is the last meal of the day but if the younger ones go out, perhaps to the cinema or just to meet friends for a drink, there is sure to be one final snack – a trip to *Pratuname*, a clothes and food market, with the food on sale day and night. Sitting under a canvas awning, beneath a line of brilliant lights it is time for one last bowl of soup noodle before bed. It is just after midnight and the heavy trucks, fancifully decorated with chrome cut-outs, are beginning to rumble in from the countryside. On top of a peak of rice sacks a young boy is curled up, fast asleep, no doubt dreaming about the City of Angels he will find when he wakes.

RICE SOUP
Khao Tom Moo

This is a standard Thai breakfast – a soup made from the previous evening's rice. It is very filling so it cannot really be served as part of a full meal. The taste is pleasantly savoury, but as it lacks the punch of much Thai food we think of it as rather bland and often use it as invalid food.

2 tbs/30ml oil
2 garlic cloves, finely chopped
16fl oz/475ml chicken stock/broth
1 tsp/5ml preserved radish (*tang chi*, p. 39)
1 tbs/15ml light soy sauce
¼ tsp/1.25ml ground white pepper
1 tbs/15ml fish sauce
2oz/60g minced/ground pork
8 oz/240g/1 cup cooked rice
coriander leaves, to garnish

In a frying pan/skillet heat the oil; fry the garlic until golden brown and set aside. In a saucepan, heat the stock with the preserved radish. Add the soy sauce, pepper and fish sauce. Bring to simmering point. Holding the minced pork loosely in one hand, pull off small pieces with the other hand and drop into the stock. When all is added, cook for a minute. Add the cooked rice and stir thoroughly; cook for 4-5 minutes until the rice is heated through and soft. The soup should be quite thick. Ladle into individual bowls, add one teaspoon each of the garlic and oil mixture, and garnish with coriander leaves.

CHICKEN, COCONUT AND GALANGAL SOUP
Gai Tom Ka

This and the following soup are far from bland. Unlike the gentle consommés in the last chapter, which are meant to counterbalance the more fiery dishes, these are vividly flavoured. The taste of lemon grass and galangal are uniquely Thai, and these soups are among the most requested dishes in my restaurant – many people often return simply because of them. They are probably too strongly flavoured to be drunk alone as a separate soup course: we would take a spoonful from time to time to flavour the rice. With these soups you have crossed the border, from elementary oriental cookery into classical Thai cuisine.

16fl oz/475ml stock/broth
2 lime leaves, chopped
2in/5cm piece lemon grass, chopped
1in/2.5cm piece galangal, split lengthways into several pieces
4 tbs/60ml fish sauce
3 tbs/45ml lemon juice
4oz/120g chicken breast, finely sliced
5fl oz/150ml coconut milk
2 small red chillies, slightly crushed
coriander leaves, to garnish

In a saucepan, heat the stock and add the lime leaves, lemon grass, galangal, fish sauce and lemon juice. Stirring thoroughly, bring to the boil. Add the chicken and the coconut milk. Continue to cook over a high heat, stirring constantly, until the meat is cooked through (about 2 minutes). Add the crushed chilli for the last few seconds. Pour into small bowls, garnish with coriander leaves and serve.

HOT AND SOUR SOUP WITH PRAWN
Tom Yam Gung

Other seafood could be used in this dish, for example mussels, scallops or crab claws. This method of preparing a hot and sour soup can also be used with finely-sliced chicken or thin slices of beef.

16fl oz/475ml stock/broth
1 tbs/15ml *tom yam* sauce (see p. 80)
2 lime leaves, chopped
2in/5cm piece lemon grass, chopped
3 tbs/45ml lemon juice
3 tbs/45ml fish sauce
1-2 (according to taste) small red or green chillies, finely chopped
½ tsp/2.5ml sugar
8 straw mushrooms, halved
8oz/450g raw prawns, peeled and deveined

In a saucepan, heat the stock and *tom yam* sauce. Add the lime leaves, lemon grass, lemon juice, fish sauce, chillies and sugar. Bring to the boil and simmer for 2 minutes. Add the mushrooms and prawns, stir and cook for 2-3 minutes until the prawns are cooked through. Serve either in a tureen or in small soup bowls.

Opposite: Two soups: Tom Yam Gung, *Hot and sour soup with prawn, and* Gai Tom Ka, *Chicken, coconut and galangal soup*

Bangkok by night

Tom yam sauce or *Nam prik pow* can be bought already prepared in small jars sometimes labelled 'Chillies in Oil'. But you can also make your own.

4 tbs/60 ml oil
3 tbs/45ml finely chopped garlic
3 tbs/45ml finely chopped shallot
3 tbs/45ml coarsely chopped long red dried chillies, deseeded
1 tbs/15ml dried prawn
1 tbs/15ml fish sauce
2tsp/10ml sugar

In a small frying pan, heat the oil, add the garlic and fry until golden brown. Remove with slotted spoon and set aside. Add the shallot to the oil and fry until golden and crisp; remove with slotted spoon and set aside. Add the chillies, fry until they start to darken then remove from the oil. Using a pestle and mortar or grinder, pound or grind the dried prawn, then add the chillies, the reserved garlic and the shallot in that order. Continue until all are thoroughly blended. Over low heat, return the blended ingredients to the original oil and warm through, stirring, to make a paste. Add the fish sauce and mix, and then the sugar. The result should be a thick, slightly oily, black/red sauce, not a paste. You can modify the chilli-heat by adding more fish sauce and sugar if you wish.

HOT AND SOUR VERMICELLI SALAD
Yam Wun Sen

Thai salads aren't collections of raw vegetables with a dressing added at the last moment, like Western ones. We use plain lettuce or crudités to garnish most savoury dishes, and a salad for us is usually a mix of bland crisp leaves with a spiced centrepiece, sometimes of marinated meat or fish, or, as in this case, of clear noodles with a highly-flavoured liquid. We like to serve piquant salads like this before the meal proper starts while we have a pre-dinner drink.

lettuce and parsley, to garnish
1 tbs/15ml oil
1 garlic clove, finely chopped
4 tbs/60ml stock/broth or water, plus extra if necessary
3 tbs/45ml lemon juice
2 tbs/30ml fish sauce
2oz/60g diced pork
4 large raw prawns, shelled and deveined
½ tsp/2.5ml chilli powder
1 tsp/5ml sugar
6-8 pieces dried mushroom, soaked in water for 20 minutes until soft, drained and halved
4oz/120g dry *Wun Sen* noodles (p. 86), soaked in water for 20 minutes until soft and drained
2 shallots, finely sliced
1 spring onion/scallion, chopped
1 sprig coriander leaves, coarsely chopped

Line a serving dish with lettuce and parsley. In a small frying pan, heat the oil and fry the garlic until golden brown. Set aside. In a saucepan, heat the stock or water, lemon juice and fish sauce, and bring to the boil. Add the pork, stir, and cook through until the meat is opaque – about 30 seconds – making sure the small pieces of meat are quite separate. Add the prawns and stir; add the chilli powder and sugar, stir and cook for about 15-20 seconds until the prawns are opaque and cooked through. Add a little more stock or water if necessary – you should have about 6-8 tbs/90-120ml liquid. Add the mushrooms, noodles, shallots and spring onion. Stir to mix thoroughly and cook for a few seconds, stirring continually, to make sure the noodles are cooked through and hot. Turn onto the prepared dish and garnish with the reserved garlic oil and chopped coriander leaves.

Opposite: Nam Prik, the author's mother's style

STEAMED SPARE-RIBS WITH BLACK BEAN
Grat Doo Moo Nueng Dow Jeow

Like the spare-rib recipe in the last chapter, this is also a very different sort of spare-rib recipe. Because the meat is steamed its flavour is rather bland, and this works well with the extreme saltiness of the black beans.

2lbs/1kg small (young) pork spare ribs, chopped into small pieces (about 1in/2.5cm) (ask your butcher to prepare them)

1 tsp/5ml salt

1 tbs/15ml sugar

2 tsp/10ml black bean sauce

2 garlic cloves, finely chopped

2 tsp/10ml flour

2 long chillies (1 red and 1 green), finely sliced

Soak the rib pieces in cold water for about half an hour to soften the meat. Drain and pat dry. In a large bowl mix the rib pieces with the rest of the ingredients, making sure each piece is coated with the mixture. Divide the mixture between 4-6 small serving bowls. Using your largest steamer (or largest pan containing enough upturned bowls to support all the bowls of ribs) steam the ribs in the bowls for 20-25 minutes and serve. (Depending on the size of your steamer and your bowls, you may have to do this in batches, keeping the first batch warm.)

PORK WITH BAMBOO SHOOTS
Normai Pad Kai

Another mild dish to balance against the hotter and spicier recipes.

2 tbs/30ml oil

1 garlic clove, finely chopped

6oz/180g lean pork, finely sliced

1 egg

2oz/60g canned bamboo shoots, sliced

2oz/60g canned straw mushrooms, halved

2 tbs/30ml light soy sauce

1 tbs/15ml fish sauce

½ tsp/2.5ml sugar

½ tsp/2.5ml ground white pepper

2 spring onions/scallions, chopped

In a wok or frying pan, heat the oil until a light haze appears. Add the garlic and fry until golden brown. Add the pork and stir over the heat for a few seconds until the meat starts to become opaque. Break the egg into the pan and mix thoroughly, scraping the egg from the sides of the wok as it cooks. Stirring quickly after each addition, add the bamboo shoots, straw mushrooms, soy sauce, fish sauce, sugar and pepper. Continue to stir over the heat until the meat is thoroughly cooked through. Add the chopped spring onions, stir to mix in, and turn out onto a serving dish.

FLAMBÉD BEEF
Nua Oh Cha

1 tsp/5ml yellow bean sauce

1 small red chilli, chopped

1 tsp/5ml mashed red bean curd

1 tbs/15ml light soy sauce

½ lb/225g rump steak, thinly sliced into 1½-2in/3-5cm long strips

2 tbs/30ml oil

2 tbs/30ml Mekong whisky (or Scotch whisky)

In a bowl, mix together the yellow bean sauce, chilli, red bean curd and light soy sauce. Add the beef and stir well, making sure that each piece is coated with the mixture. Allow to stand for at least half an hour.

In a wok or frying pan, heat the oil until a light haze appears. Fry the marinated beef, stirring, for about 2 minutes over a high heat. Turn onto a serving dish and pour the whisky over the meat. Set the whisky alight (flambé) and serve as soon as the flame has gone out.

BEEF WITH LIME LEAVES AND CHILLI
Nua Pad Ki Mow

3 tbs/45ml oil

2 garlic cloves, finely chopped

1 medium-size red chilli, finely chopped

6oz/180g beef, finely sliced

1 tbs/15ml light soy sauce

1 tbs/15ml fish sauce

¼ tsp/1.5ml sugar

2 lime leaves, finely sliced

4 tbs/60ml stock/broth

¼ red pepper, finely slivered

2-4 green beans, cut diagonally into 1½in/4cm pieces

¼ tsp/1.5ml ground white pepper

In a wok or frying pan/skillet, heat the oil until a light haze appears. Fry the garlic until golden brown. Add the chilli and stir quickly. Add the beef and stir thoroughly. Add the soy sauce, fish sauce, sugar, lime leaves and stock. Cook for a minute or two over a high heat, stirring all the time and mixing thoroughly. Add the red pepper, green beans and white pepper and stir for 4-5 seconds. Turn onto a serving dish.

STUFFED OMELETTE
Kai Yat Sy

Although we call this an omelette it is really more like a filled crêpe. The taste leans towards sweetness so it must be served with something very savoury, such as the preceding beef dish. Taste aside, the real pleasure of this omelette is its unusual box-shape from which its colourful contents spill out when it is cut. It is worth having one or two practice runs at this dish to make sure it will succeed and impress your guests. It is easier to make in a wok than in a frying pan.

Filling:
1 tbs/15ml oil
1 garlic clove, finely chopped
2oz/60g minced/ground pork
about 1 tbs finely chopped carrot
about 1 tbs finely chopped onion
about 1 tbs finely chopped green beans
about 1 tbs finely chopped sweet red pepper
about 1 tbs finely chopped green pepper
1 small tomato, finely chopped
1 tbs/15ml peas (frozen will do)
2 tbs/30ml fish sauce
1 tbs/15ml light soy sauce
1 tbs/15ml tomato ketchup/catsup
½ tsp/2.5ml ground white pepper
Omelette:
2 eggs
1 tbs/15ml fish sauce
ground white pepper
1 tbs/15ml oil
coriander leaves and slivers of red and green pepper, to garnish

Make the filling. In a wok, heat the oil, add the garlic and fry until golden brown. Add the pork, and fry until the meat is white and opaque. Quickly add all the chopped vegetables and stir once. Add the fish sauce, soy sauce, tomato ketchup and pepper, and stir-fry over a high heat for 1 minute. Turn the mixture into a dish and set aside.

Clean the wok with kitchen paper. In a small bowl lightly beat the eggs with the fish sauce and a shake of white pepper. Heat the oil in the wok, tilting it over the heat to cover the inner surface with a fine film of hot oil. Add the beaten egg and tilt the wok to cover as much of the inner surface as possible with a thin layer of the egg mixture. Leave to cook for a few seconds to form a 'crêpe' and, when it is firm enough to hold its shape, tip the reserved filling into the centre. With a spatula fold the sides of the crêpe over the filling to form a square package. Slide onto a serving plate and garnish with coriander leaves and red and green pepper slivers.

MILLION-YEAR-EGGS
Tom Kem

This is that rare thing, a Thai stew – a dish that actually improves for being kept and re-heated. When I was a student in London it was one of the few Thai dishes I could find the ingredients for and I used to produce it in large quantities. Seeing it come back time and again my friends dubbed it 'million-year-eggs', the name I have given it here. It is obviously a useful standby and good for parties.

5 garlic cloves, finely chopped
2 coriander roots, finely chopped
½ tsp/2.5ml coarsely ground black pepper
1 tbs/15ml oil
1½lbs/700g belly pork cut into 1in/2.5cm cubes
1½-2pts/750-950ml stock/broth or water
2 tbs/30ml dark soy sauce
3 tbs/95ml fish sauce
2 tbs/30ml sugar
6 hard-boiled/cooked eggs, shelled
4 × 1in/2.5cm cubes fried bean curd (p.37), halved
Serves 6

Pound together the garlic, coriander roots and ground black pepper in a pestle and mortar, or grind in a blender. In a large heavy saucepan heat the oil and fry this mixture for 1 minute. Add the chunks of pork and fry for a minute or two, turning the pieces to absorb some of the mixture. Add enough stock or water to cover the mixture by 1in/2.5cm and bring to the boil. Skim off any impurities that come to the surface. Add the soy sauce, fish sauce and sugar. Add the hard-boiled eggs and simmer gently for an hour, skimming if necessary. The eggs should acquire a dark brown colour. Add the bean curd and cook for a few minutes longer.

A well-fed traffic warden, Bangkok

NAM PRIK, MY MOTHER'S STYLE
Nam Prik Kapee

Nam prik (literally, 'hot' or spicy water) is a Thai staple; a liquid paste into which raw vegetables, cold cooked vegetables and deep-fried fish are dipped and eaten with rice. This is another of those real tastes of Thailand, and is based on fermented ingredients which have a pungent smell that the newcomer may find unappealing. It's a question of holding your nose and eating – once you enjoy the taste you'll ignore the smell.

Every region of Thailand has its own versions of *Nam prik*, and indeed every Thai cook has his or her own special recipe – there will be others later on in this book. Traditionally, a Thai lady made her *Nam prik* while her servants got on with the main cooking, so the dish has acquired the status of an offering even though it is eaten frequently and isn't reserved for special occasions. The pea aubergines/eggplant we use in this sauce are rarely available in the West; they really are the size of peas or small marbles. You could use larger aubergines, 1-1½in/2.5-4cm in diameter, instead, but they are not essential.

This recipe is my mother's favourite.

2 garlic cloves, chopped
5 small hot chillies
1 tbs/15ml shrimp paste
3 tbs/45ml fish sauce
3 tbs/45ml lemon juice
1 tbs/15ml sugar
2 tbs/30ml crushed pea aubergines/eggplant, if available
To serve:
crudités (French/snap beans cut into 2in/5cm lengths, slivers of carrot, celery and cucumber) or
1 pomphret or 3 fresh sardines, cleaned (if available), plus oil for deep frying

Using a pestle and mortar or a blender, pound the garlic with the chillies. Gently grill the shrimp paste for 2 or 3 minutes (this may not be necessary in the West but we do it to destroy any bacteria that may have developed in our much hotter weather). Add the shrimp paste to the garlic and chilli mixture, blend, then add the rest of the ingredients and mix thoroughly. Serve with crudités. If you have a pomphret or sardines, deep fry the former and grill/broil the latter until quite dry and crisp, so that diners can scrape the flesh from the spine to dip in the *Nam prik*.

NOODLES/GUEYTEOW

This is the branch of Thai cuisine closest to Chinese cooking. If it is true that Marco Polo took the idea of pasta back to Italy, then he rather lost his sense of time on the long journey home, for whereas spaghetti, fuselli, etc. take several minutes to cook, oriental noodles take seconds. The time-consuming part is preparing all the other ingredients before you start so that they are ready literally to be flung into the pan for the small amount of cooking required.

There are five varieties of noodle, four made from rice flour and one from soya-bean flour. In most Thai noodle dishes, the protein element comes in the form of pre-prepared meat or fish balls. All these ingredients, both noodles and prepared meats, are available in Chinese stores and are exactly the same as those used in Thailand, where buying ready-made ingredients of this sort is standard practice.

Some Chinese supermarkets now stock fresh noodles which, especially in the case of egg noodles, are an improvement on the dried variety. The only difference in cooking is that the dried noodles should be soaked in water for a short time before they are used.

Apart from dividing by variety of noodle used, these dishes can be separated into dry and wet ones; that is, into fried noodle dishes or soup noodle dishes. A standard Thai lunch is often a bowl of soup noodle followed by a bowl of fried noodle. In some cases, soup noodle is made simply by adding stock/broth to the dry noodle.

The most famous dish of all is Pad Thai – a fried noodle with a complex set of ingredients that are mixed together by the diner. The flavour of Pad Thai is one of the most evocative in Thai cuisine and this gives it some claim to be the national dish.

FIVE NOODLES

1. Sen Yai Sometimes called River Rice Noodle or Rice Sticks, this is a broad, flat, white noodle. Bought fresh, it is rather sticky and the strands usually need to be separated by hand before cooking. Can also be bought dried.

2. Sen Lek A medium flat noodle, about $\frac{1}{10}$ in/2mm wide, and usually sold dried.

Making fresh river rice noodles

3. Sen Mee A small wiry-looking rice noodle, usually sold dried, sometimes called 'rice vermicelli'.

4. Ba Mee An egg noodle, medium yellow in colour, which can be bought fresh in 'nests'; these need to be shaken loose by hand before cooking.

5. Wun Sen A very thin, very wiry, transparent soya-bean-flour noodle, called either vermicelli, or 'cellophane noodle'. Only available dried.

All dried noodles need to be soaked in cold water for about 20 minutes before cooking; (vermicelli will usually require less soaking). They are quickly drained in a sieve or colander, and then cooked; usually a matter of simply dunking them into boiling water for 2-3 seconds. The dry weight will usually double after soaking, ie. 4oz/120g dry noodles are equivalent to 8oz/230g soaked noodles.

FOUR FLAVOURS
Kruang Prung

While each noodle dish has a distinctive flavour of its own, the final taste is left very much up to the consumer. When eating noodles in Thailand, it is standard practice to offer a set of four flavours: chillies in fish sauce/*Nam Pla Prik* (4 small green or red chillies to 4 tbs/60ml fish sauce), chopped chillies in rice vinegar/*Prik Nam Som* (4 small green or red chillies to 4 tbs/60ml vinegar), sugar/*Nam Tan* and red chilli powder/*Prik Pon*, so that the dish can be adjusted as the diner wishes.

RIVER NOODLES WITH PORK AND DARK SOY
Pad Si Yew

1 tbs/15ml oil
2 garlic cloves, finely chopped
4oz/120g minced/ground lean pork
1 egg
8oz/230g (wet weight) soaked *Sen Yai* noodles (p. 85)
2oz/60g broccoli, coarsely chopped
1 tbs/15ml dark soy sauce
1 tbs/15ml light soy sauce
pinch of sugar
2 tbs/30ml fish sauce
ground white pepper
chilli powder (optional)

Heat the oil in a wok or frying pan over a high heat. Add the garlic and fry until golden brown. Add the pork, stir, and cook briefly until the meat is opaque. Break the egg into the mixture, stir, and cook quickly. Add the noodles and stir quickly; add the broccoli and stir again to blend. Stirring quickly after each addition, add the dark soy, the light soy, the sugar, and the fish sauce. Give the mixture a final stir, turn onto a serving dish, shake the ground white pepper over, and the chilli powder if liked, and serve.

PORK AND FISH BALL NOODLES
Gueyteow Heng Moo

This is quite bland, and *must* be served with side dishes of the four flavours.

2 tbs/30ml oil
2 garlic cloves, finely chopped
1 tsp/5ml preserved radish (*tang chi*, p. 39)
1 tbs/15ml fish sauce
1 tbs/15ml light soy sauce
½ tsp/2.5ml sugar
1oz/30g beansprouts
8oz/230g (wet weight) soaked *Sen Yai* noodles (p. 85), rinsed and separated
3 prepared pork balls
3 prepared fish balls
4 slices prepared fish cake
4 slices cold boiled pork
1 tbs/15ml crushed roasted peanuts, plus extra to serve if wished
1 sprig of coriander leaves, coarsely chopped

Heat the oil in a small frying pan, add the garlic and fry until golden brown. Set aside. Put the preserved radish, fish sauce, soy sauce and sugar into a deep serving bowl, mix quickly and set aside. Bring a large pan of water to the boil. Using a wire-meshed ladle or a small coarse sieve with a handle, dip the beansprouts into the boiling water for a count of three – enough to heat through. Turn the beansprouts into the serving bowl. Next, dip the noodles into the hot water in the same way, but shake them slightly in the water – again, only for a few seconds. Add to the serving bowl and pour over them 1 tbs/15ml of the reserved garlic and oil (this helps to separate the noodles as well as adding flavour). In turn, dip the pork balls, the fish balls and the fish cake into the hot water, heating them through for a few seconds before adding to the bowl. Arrange the slices of cold pork (without heating them) on the noodles. Sprinkle the dish with the crushed peanuts and the chopped coriander leaves. Serve, having first tossed the whole dish together quickly. Accompany with the four flavours and additional peanuts if wished.

To turn this dish into a noodle soup, simply pour on ¾pt/475ml hot stock/broth before garnishing with the peanuts and coriander leaves.

MINCED BEEF NOODLE WITH CURRY POWDER
Gueyteow Nua Sap

| lettuce, to serve |
| 2 tbs/30ml oil |
| 8oz/230g (wet weight) soaked Sen Yai noodles (p. 85), rinsed and separated |
| about 1½ tbs/22ml dark soy sauce |
| 1 garlic clove, finely chopped |
| 4oz/120g minced/ground lean beef |
| 1 tbs/15ml preserved radish (tang chi, p. 39) |
| ¼pt/125ml stock/broth (with a little more to hand if necessary) |
| ½ tbs/7.5ml curry powder |
| 1 small onion, finely slivered |
| 1 tbs/15ml fish sauce |
| 1 tbs/15ml flour mixed to a thin paste with water (this may be a little more than required) |
| 1 small spring onion/scallion, finely chopped |
| 1 sprig coriander leaves, coarsely chopped |

Line a serving dish with coarsely torn lettuce.

Heat 1 tbs/15ml oil in a wok or frying pan/skillet. Add the noodles, stir quickly and add half a tablespoon dark soy. Stir for 30-60 seconds to prevent sticking. Turn onto the prepared serving dish. Heat 1 tbs/15ml more oil, add the garlic and fry until golden brown. Add the beef, stir and cook quickly until beef loses its red colour. Add the remaining ingredients including the remaining soy sauce one by one, stirring briefly after each addition. (The flour and water paste will thicken the sauce: add only a teaspoonful at a time). Add a little more stock if the mixture becomes too dry. Turn the beef mixture onto the noodles and serve.

FRIED NOODLES WITH CHICKEN
Gueyteow Pad Gai

Again, the cooking time of this recipe is very brief, only a minute or two, and success depends on speed.

| lettuce, to garnish |
| 1 tbs/15ml oil |
| 1 garlic clove, finely chopped |
| 4oz/120g boneless chicken, finely sliced |
| 1 egg |
| 1 tsp/5ml preserved radish (tang chi, p. 39) |
| 8oz/230g (wet weight) soaked Sen Lek noodles (p. 85) |
| 1 tbs/15ml light soy sauce |
| pinch of sugar |
| 1 tbs/15ml fish sauce |
| 1 large spring onion/scallion, chopped |
| shaking of ground white pepper |
| sprig of coriander leaf, coarsely chopped, to garnish |

Line a serving dish with roughly torn lettuce. Heat the oil in a wok or frying pan. Add the garlic and fry until golden brown. Add the chicken and stir until the meat is white and opaque. Break the egg into the wok or pan and stir quickly. Add the remaining ingredients, one by one, stirring quickly after each addition, and making sure the noodles do not stick to the pan. Turn the mixture onto the serving dish and garnish with the coriander.

SPICY BEEF NOODLES WITH LIME LEAF

Gueyteow Pad Ki Mow

1 tbs/15ml oil
1 garlic clove, finely chopped
1-2 small chillies, finely chopped (about 1 tsp/15ml)
½ tsp/2.5ml chilli powder
4oz/120g lean beef, thinly sliced
1 tbs/15ml fish sauce
1 tbs/15ml dark soy sauce
½ tsp/2.5ml sugar
2 lime leaves, finely sliced
1 medium tomato, chopped
8oz/230g (wet weight) soaked *Sen Yai* noodles (p. 85), rinsed and separated
sprig of coriander leaves, coarsely chopped, to garnish

Heat the oil in a wok or frying pan. Add the garlic, stir, and fry until golden brown. Add the fresh chilli and the chilli powder, and stir for 2 seconds, then add the beef and stir in well. Add the fish sauce, soy sauce, sugar and lime leaves, one by one, stirring quickly after each addition. Add the tomato, stir until cooked, and then add the noodles. Stir over the heat briefly until cooked through. Turn onto the serving dish and garnish with coriander leaves.

PORK AND VEGETABLE NOODLES WITH BLACK BEANS

Sen Mee Lahd Nah

2 tbs/30ml oil
8oz/230g (wet weight) soaked *Sen Mee* noodles (p. 85)
3 tbs/45ml light soy sauce
1 garlic clove, finely chopped
4oz/120g lean pork, finely sliced
1 tbs/15ml fish sauce
about 4 tbs/60ml stock/broth or water (have more to hand)
1 tsp/5ml black bean sauce

Opposite: Pad Thai, the classic Thai fried noodle dish, combining many different flavours from chopped peanuts to dried prawns, that has some claim to be the national dish. Readily available from countless stalls on every city street and in every village market

1 tbs/15ml flour mixed with 2 tbs/30ml water to make a thin paste (this will give more than you need)
4oz/60g mixed green vegetables (spring greens, mangetout/snow peas, broccoli etc.)
½ tsp/5ml sugar
¼ tsp/1.5ml ground white pepper

In a wok or frying pan, heat 1 tbs/15ml oil. Add the noodles and stir quickly, then add 1 tbs/15ml light soy sauce and stir for 30-60 seconds to avoid sticking. Turn onto a serving dish. Add another 1 tbs/15ml oil to the wok, heat, add garlic and fry until golden brown. Add the pork, stir and cook until the meat is white and opaque, add the fish sauce and the remaining soy sauce and stir. Add a little stock and the black bean sauce. Stir. Add 4 tsp/20ml of the flour and water mixture and stir in thoroughly. Stir in the vegetables and sugar. Cook for a few seconds, stirring all the time then shake the pepper over. Stir once, then turn onto the noodles.

FRIED EGG NOODLES WITH CHICKEN AND BAMBOO SHOOTS

Ba Mee Lahd Nah

1 nest *Ba Mee* noodles (p. 86), fresh or dry
2 tbs/30ml oil
2 garlic cloves, finely chopped
4oz/120g boneless chicken, finely sliced
2oz/60g bamboo shoots, sliced
8-10 straw mushrooms, halved
1 tbs/15ml light soy sauce
1 tbs/15ml dark soy sauce
2 tbs/30ml fish sauce
pinch of sugar
4 tbs/60ml stock/broth
white pepper
1 tbs/15ml flour mixed with 2tbs/30ml water
1 spring onion/scallion, coarsely chopped

If using fresh noodles, shake the strands loose. Bring a pan of water to the boil. Using a coarse-meshed strainer or a sieve, dip the noodles into the boiling water. If using fresh noodles leave in for a few seconds until cooked through; if using dry, leave in until the strands have softened. Drain.

In a wok or frying pan, heat 1 tbs/15ml oil and fry half the garlic until golden brown. Add the noodles and stir briefly until slightly darker and no longer wet. Turn onto a serving dish. Heat the remaining 1 tbs/15ml oil and fry the remaining garlic until golden brown. Add

Loo Chin Tod, *skewers of beef balls deep fried and sold in little plastic bags with a sweet and hot chilli sauce. A favourite afternoon snack*

stir-fry briefly until the meat is opaque. Add the fish sauce and 1 tbs/15ml soy sauce and stir. Break the eggs into the pan, mix and spread the egg over the cooking surface to cook a little. Add the drained vermicelli and mix thoroughly. Add the remaining 1 tbs/15ml soy sauce, the stock, onion and mushrooms and stir quickly to mix well. Add the spring onions, sugar and sprinkling of pepper, stir once more and turn onto a serving dish.

the chicken and cook until the meat is opaque. Add the bamboo shoots and straw mushrooms and stir. Add the light soy, dark soy, fish sauce, sugar, stock and a sprinkling of pepper, stirring briefly after each addition. Add enough flour and water to thicken the mixture slightly and cook for a minute or two. Add the spring onion, stir, and turn onto the noodles.

FRIED VERMICELLI WITH PORK AND SPRING ONIONS/SCALLIONS
Moo Pad Wun Sen

Usually, this dish is not served as a separate noodle course but as part of a main meal.

2oz/60g dry *Wun Sen* noodles (p. 86), soaked in cold water for 15 minutes
2 tbs/30ml oil
1 garlic clove, finely chopped
4oz/120g lean pork, finely sliced
1 tbs/15ml fish sauce
2 tbs/30ml light soy sauce
2 eggs
2 tbs/30ml stock/broth or water
1 small onion, slivered
6-8 dried mushrooms soaked in cold water until soft (about 15 minutes), and cut if necessary
2 spring onions/scallions, trimmed and cut into 1½in/4cm pieces
½ tsp/2.5ml sugar
ground white pepper

Drain the vermicelli ready for cooking. Heat the oil in a wok or frying pan. Add the garlic and fry until golden brown. Add the pork and

VERMICELLI IN SOUP WITH RED BEAN SAUCE
Suki Gai

4 oz/120g boneless chicken, diced
1 tbs/15ml light soy sauce
1 tbs/15ml fish sauce
1 egg, lightly beaten
¼ tsp/1.5ml sugar
shaking of ground white pepper
Sauce:
1 tbs/15ml red bean curd
1 tbs/15ml lemon juice
½ tsp/2.5ml chilli powder
½ tsp/2.5ml fish sauce
½ tsp/2.5ml light soy sauce
1 tsp/5ml sugar
1 tsp/5ml finely chopped pickled garlic (see p.98)
Soup:
1pt/2½ cups/570ml stock/broth
2oz/60g Chinese leaves, coarsely chopped
2oz/60g celery (with some leaf), chopped
2 spring onions/scallions, chopped diagonally
1 tbs/15ml fish sauce
1 tbs/15ml soy sauce
2oz/60g dry *Wun Sen* noodles p. 86, soaked in water for 15 minutes

Originally a breakfast snack, pigeon's eggs cooked on a griddle at the edge of a market

Duck farm outside Bangkok to supply the restaurants of Chinatown

In a small bowl mix the first six ingredients together and set aside. Combine the sauce ingredients in a bowl and whisk/beat with a fork until smooth. Set aside.

In a saucepan bring the stock quickly to the boil. Add the reserved chicken mixture, stir quickly and cook for 1 or 2 minutes until the meat is opaque. Add the vegetables, fish sauce and soy sauce, and stir. Add the vermicelli, still stirring, and cook for 2 or 3 seconds: the noodles become soft very quickly. Turn into a bowl. Serve the sauce separately as it has a strong flavour: allow each diner to stir it in as required (I suggest you start with ½ tsp/ 2.5ml).

THAI FRIED NOODLES
Pad Thai

The total cooking time for this dish shouldn't exceed 2-3 minutes.

4 tbs/60ml oil
2 garlic cloves, finely chopped
1 egg
4 oz/120g dry *Sen Lek* noodles (p. 85), soaked in water for 20 minutes until soft, and drained
2 tbs/30ml lemon juice
1½ tbs/22.5ml fish sauce
½ tsp/2.5ml sugar
2 tbs/30ml chopped roast peanuts
2tbs/30ml dried shrimp, ground or pounded
½ tsp/2.5ml chilli powder
1 tbs/15ml finely chopped preserved turnip (*chi po*, p. 38)
1oz/30g beansprouts
2 spring onions/scallions, chopped into 1in/2.5cm pieces
sprig of coriander leaf, coarsely chopped
lemon wedges, to garnish

In a wok or frying pan, heat the oil, add the garlic and fry until golden brown. Break the egg into the wok, stir quickly and cook for a couple of seconds. Add the noodles and stir well, scraping down the sides of the pan to ensure they mix with the garlic and egg. One by one, add the lemon juice, fish sauce, sugar, half the peanuts, half the dried shrimp, the chilli powder, the preserved turnip, 1 table-spoon of the beansprouts, and the spring onions, stirring quickly all the time. Test the noodles for tenderness. When done, turn onto a serving plate and arrange the remaining peanuts, dried shrimp and beansprouts around the dish. Garnish with the coriander and lemon wedges.

CURRY/KARI

Chillies drying in the sun with stone mortars ready for pounding

Earlier, I mentioned the Thai tradition of making curry pastes at home rather than buying them. While this is time-consuming it is well worth the effort. I find it easier to spend a whole day making several pastes at once, all of which will be used in the coming two or three weeks.

In Thailand, we would use a heavy stone pestle and mortar for making curry pastes. As a substitute, I suggest you use either an electric coffee-grinder (because of the pungent flavours you will have to keep a grinder uniquely for this purpose), or buy pre-ground spices, such as coriander, cumin, etc. and use an electric blender to mix them in. If you want to try your hand at the traditional method, I suggest you pound all the 'hard' ingredients (cloves, coriander and cumin seeds, star anise, etc.) first, as these take most effort, and then add the remaining ingredients. There are many Thai curries; here I have chosen four that are very different in taste. After explaining the pastes, I give examples of how to use them: substitute other meats and vegetables for those I have suggested if you prefer.

Unlike Indian curries, Thai ones do not require long cooking, only a few minutes once the ingredients are prepared and ready to hand – like all Thai dishes. Our curries are also less 'thickened' than Indian ones; they are often more like a heavily spiced soup than a savoury dish. Ready-made curry pastes can be bought in Chinese and oriental stores. They make a convenient alternative, but are never as good as the homemade variety.

If you are using whole seeds to obtain the ground powder, first grind these separately in a blender or coffee grinder.

GREEN CURRY PASTE
Gaeng Kiow Wan

2 long green chillies, chopped

10 small green chillies, chopped

1 tbs/15ml chopped lemon grass

3 shallots, chopped

2 tbs/30 ml chopped garlic (about 4 cloves)

1in/2.5cm piece galangal, chopped

3 coriander roots, chopped

1 tsp/5ml ground coriander seed

½ tsp/2.5ml ground cumin

½ tsp/2.5ml ground white pepper

1 tsp/5ml chopped kaffir lime skin (p. 38) or finely chopped lime leaves (p. 36)

2 tsp/10ml shrimp paste

1 tsp/5ml salt

Using a pestle and mortar or a grinder, blend all the ingredients together until they form a smooth paste. These amounts will yield about 3 tbs/45ml paste.

RED CURRY PASTE
Gaeng Pet

8 dried long red chillies, deseeded and chopped
1 tsp/5ml ground coriander seed
½ tsp/2.5ml ground cumin seed
1 tsp/5ml ground white pepper
2 tbs/30ml chopped garlic (about 4 cloves)
2 stalks lemon grass, finely chopped
3 coriander roots, chopped
1 tsp/5ml chopped kaffir lime skin (p. 38) or finely chopped lime leaves
1in/2.5cm piece galangal, chopped
2 tsp/10ml shrimp paste
1 tsp/5ml salt

Using a pestle and mortar or grinder, blend all the ingredients together to make a smooth paste. You should have about 4 tbs/60ml paste.

DRY CURRY PASTE
Panaeng

10 dried long red chillies, deseeded and chopped
5 shallots, chopped
2 tbs/30ml chopped garlic (about 4 cloves)
2 stalks lemon grass, chopped
1in/2.5cm piece galangal, chopped
1 tsp/5ml ground coriander seed
1 tsp/5ml ground cumin
3 coriander roots, chopped
1 tsp/5ml shrimp paste
2 tbs/30ml roasted peanuts

Using a pestle and mortar or a grinder, blend all the ingredients together until they form a smooth paste. You should have about 6 tbs/90ml paste.

MASSAMAN PASTE
Massaman

10 dried long red chillies, deseeded and chopped
1 tbs/15ml ground coriander seed
1 tsp/5ml ground cumin
1 tsp/5ml ground cinnamon
1 tsp/5ml ground cloves
1 tsp/5ml ground star anise
1 tsp/5ml ground cardamom
1 tsp/5ml ground white pepper
4 tbs/60ml chopped shallots (about 6 shallots)

4 tbs/60 ml chopped garlic (about 7 cloves)
about 2 in/5cm piece lemon grass, chopped
½ in/1.25cm piece galangal, chopped
1 tbs/15ml chopped kaffir lime skin (p. 38) or chopped lime leaves
1 tbs/15ml shrimp paste
1 tbs/15ml salt

Blend the chillies, coriander, cumin, cinnamon, cloves, star anise, cardamom and white pepper together. Add the rest of the ingredients, one by one, blending after each addition, until you have a smooth paste. You should have about 6 tbs/90 ml paste.

GREEN BEEF CURRY
Gaeng Kiow Wan

At home this is always made with pea aubergines/eggplant. Here I have substituted the more easily-available small green aubergines.

4fl oz/125ml/½cup coconut cream
2 tbs/30ml oil
1 garlic clove, finely chopped
1 tbs/15ml Green curry paste (p. 92)
2 tbs/30ml fish sauce
1 tsp/5ml sugar
6oz/180g diced lean beef
4fl oz/125ml/½ cup stock/broth or water
2 lime leaves, chopped
3 small green aubergines/eggplant, quartered
15 holy basil leaves

In a small pan, gently heat the coconut cream. Do not boil. In a frying pan or wok, heat the oil until a light haze appears. Add the chopped garlic and fry until golden brown. Add the curry paste, and stir-fry for a few seconds. Add the warmed coconut cream and stir until it curdles and thickens in the oil. Add the fish sauce and sugar and stir. Add the beef and turn in the mixture until its red colour disappears. Add the stock or water, stir, and simmer for 3-4 minutes, stirring occasionally. Add the lime leaves, stir, then add the aubergines and basil leaves. Stir and cook for one minute more then turn into a serving dish.

Overleaf: Preparing green beef curry, Gaeng Kiow Wan. Ingredients for the paste, the finished curry with aubergines and three side dishes: salty eggs, pickled garlic and pickled cabbage

RED CHICKEN CURRY
Gaeng Pet Gai

You can substitute small green aubergines/eggplant for the bamboo shoot pieces in this dish, but these should be added before the lime leaves so that they may cook a little longer.

4fl oz/125ml/½cup coconut cream
2 tbs/30ml oil
1 garlic clove, chopped
1 tbs/15ml Red curry paste (p. 93)
2 tbs/30ml fish sauce
1 tsp/5ml sugar
6oz/180g boneless chicken, finely sliced
4fl oz/125ml/½cup stock/broth or water
2 lime leaves, chopped
½ piece of canned bamboo shoot, cut into slivers
15 holy basil leaves

In a small pan, gently heat the coconut cream but do not let it boil. In a wok or frying pan, heat the oil until a light haze appears, then add the garlic and fry until golden brown. Add the curry paste, and stir-fry for a few seconds. Add the warmed coconut cream and stir until it curdles and thickens in the oil. Add the fish sauce and sugar and stir. Add the chicken, stir, and cook until the meat is opaque. Then add the stock, stir and cook for 1-2 minutes until the meat is cooked through. Add the lime leaves and stir, then add the bamboo shoot and basil leaves. Stir and cook gently for 1 minute. Turn into serving dish.

PANAENG CURRY
Gaeng Panaeng

4fl oz/125ml/½cup coconut cream, plus 1 tbs/15ml for garnish
2 tbs/30ml oil
1 garlic clove, finely chopped
1 tbs/15ml Dry curry paste (p. 93)
2 tbs/30ml fish sauce
1 tsp/5ml sugar
6oz/180g lean beef, diced
2 lime leaves, chopped very fine
15 holy basil leaves
1 long red chilli, slivered

In a small pan, gently heat the coconut cream but do not let it boil. In a wok or frying pan, heat the oil until a light haze appears, add the garlic and fry until golden brown. Add the curry paste, and stir-fry for a few seconds. Add

A stall selling ready to eat Nam Prik pastes – some with fish, some prawn, some tamarind

A traditional coconut grater in the form of a rabbit

the warmed coconut cream (reserving 1 tbs/ 15ml for garnish), and stir until it curdles and thickens in the oil. Add the fish sauce and sugar and stir. Add the beef, stir and cook gently for 3-4 minutes. Add the lime leaves and stir in, then add the basil leaves. Cook for 1 minute. This is meant to be a dry curry, but add a little water during the cooking if you feel it is drying out too much. When the beef is cooked through, turn the mixture onto a serving dish and garnish with the reserved coconut cream and the slivers of red chilli.

THAI MUSLIM CURRY
Massaman Kari

The extreme south of Thailand, along our narrow border with Malaysia, has a largely Muslim population. From them we have acquired the satay sauce and this rich, though mild, curry. You can give it more fire by increasing the amount of paste you use. This curry needs to 'stew' a little.

8fl oz/250ml/1 cup coconut cream
2 tbs/30ml oil
1 garlic clove, finely chopped
1 tbs/15ml Massaman curry paste (p. 93)
6oz/180g lean beef, cubed
1 tbs/15ml tamarind juice, or 2 tbs/30ml lemon juice
1 tsp/5ml sugar
3 tbs/45ml fish sauce
8fl oz/250ml/1 cup stock/broth or water
2 small potatoes, quartered
2 tbs/40g roasted peanuts
2 small onions, quartered

In a small pan, gently warm the coconut cream until it just starts to separate. In a wok or frying pan/skillet, heat the oil, add the garlic and fry until golden brown. Add the curry paste, mix well and cook for a few seconds. Add half the warmed coconut cream, stir thoroughly to mix and, still stirring, cook for a further few seconds until the mixture bubbles and starts to reduce. Add the beef and turn to ensure that each piece of meat is thoroughly coated with sauce. Stirring after each addition, add the tamarind or lemon juice, sugar, fish sauce, stock or water and the remainder of the coconut cream. Stir and cook slowly for 15 minutes. Add the quartered potatoes and simmer. After 4 minutes, add the peanuts and cook for 4 minutes more. Add the onions, stir and cook for 2 more minutes. Turn into a serving dish.

SIDE-DISHES

The pickle stall in Wararot market, Chiang Mai. Not only vegetables but fruits like mango are preserved in rice vinegar

We usually balance the rich flavours of a curry with side-dishes that have lighter, sharper or sweeter tastes. You could serve 'Son-in-law eggs' (p. 61) or Pickled Cabbage (p. 62) with curries, and here are three more accompaniments.

PICKLED GARLIC
Kratiem Dong

Some of the early Western visitors to Siam were critical of the amounts of pickled garlic that were eaten. It is certainly an acquired taste and one best shared with close companions!

At home we pickle whole bulbs of garlic (which are smaller than the Western variety), and they look very pleasing in their pickling jars. Western garlic is too big for this treatment, so you will have to break it up into cloves. A little of this goes a long way.

2 large whole garlic bulbs, separated into cloves and peeled
¾pt/250ml white rice vinegar
2 tsp/10ml sugar
2 tsp/10ml salt

Place the peeled garlic cloves in a small preserving jar. Heat the vinegar with the sugar and salt until the sugar and salt are dissolved. Allow the mixture to cool. Pour the liquid over the garlic, seal the jar and leave for 1 week.

SALTY EGGS
Kai Kem

This is so easy to make and it makes a deliciously salty side-dish – the direct opposite of Son-in-law eggs.

8-9 eggs (duck eggs are preferred, but large chicken eggs are quite satisfactory)
10oz/300g/1cup salt
1¼pt/700ml/3cups water

Place the eggs, being careful not to crack the shells, in a 4pt/2l (or larger) preserving jar. Heat the salt and water together in a pan until the salt is dissolved. Allow to cool, and then pour the mixture over the eggs in the jar. Seal the jar and leave for 3 weeks after which the eggs can be boiled or fried.

SWEET CRISPY NOODLE
Mee Krop

This dish brings the noodle and curry sections together. I cannot pretend that it is anything other than a very complex dish – one of the most time-consuming in the book – but it does contain a unique blend of tastes and textures. It is the perfect accompaniment to a green or red curry, and, if you make it once I am sure you will come back to it again and again. Happily, it can be made a little in advance of a meal so that you don't have to go through all these rather finnicky stages right up to the time of eating.

oil for deep frying
4oz/120g dry *Sen Mee* noodles (p. 86), soaked in cold water for 20 minutes, and drained
Sauce:
2 tbs/30ml oil
2 × 1in/2.5cm cubes prepared fried bean curd (p. 37), cut or shredded into thin strips
2 tbs/30ml oil
2 garlic cloves, finely chopped
2 shallots, finely chopped
1oz/30g minced/ground pork
2 tbs/30ml fish sauce
4 tbs/60ml sugar
4 tbs/60ml stock/broth
3 tbs/45ml lemon juice
½ tsp/2.5ml chilli powder
Additions:
2 tbs/30ml oil
1 egg, lightly beaten with 1 tbs/15ml cold water
1oz/30g beansprouts
1 spring onion/scallion, cut into 1in/2.5cm slivers
1 medium-size red chilli, deseeded and slivered lengthways

Heat the oil in a deep-fryer until medium-hot. In two batches, fry the drained noodles until they are golden brown and crisp. Remove from the fryer, drain, and set aside.

In a wok or frying pan, heat the 2 tbs of oil, add the shredded bean curd, and fry until crispy. Remove with a slotted spoon and set aside. Reheat the oil, add the garlic and fry until golden brown; remove and set aside. Next fry the shallot until brown, remove and set aside. Then fry the pork until cooked through. Stirring, add the fish sauce, sugar, stock, and lemon juice. Stir the mixture until it begins to caramelize. Add the chilli powder and stir. Stir in the reserved bean curd, garlic and shallot, and mix until they soak up some of the sweet liquid. Set aside.

In a small pan, heat the remaining 2 tbs of oil. Drip in the egg mixture from the tips of the fingers; it will cook immediately, making little scraps of egg. Remove, drain, and set aside.

Return the wok or pan containing the sauce to the heat. Crumble the crisp vermicelli into the sauce, mix gently, and cook together briefly. Turn into a serving dish and sprinkle the beansprouts, spring onion, fried egg pieces and chilli over the mixture.

Embroidered cloth in traditional design

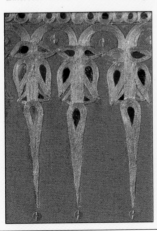

BY THE SEA

SEAFOOD

olidays at the seaside hold the same attractions for Thai children as for those of any other land: swimming, building sand-castles, beach football. I, however, always found greatest pleasure in walking alone for hours down an endless strand of white beach. I liked to stop and stare into a rock pool, watching a creature tentatively peep out of its shell, and I was always amused by the near transparent ghost-crabs scuttling sideways, as if turning cartwheels, before diving into their impossibly tiny holes in the sand. The only things which ever worried me were the giant jelly-fish, washed into the shallows during the rainy season. These monsters could be found on the beach when the tide went out and I would sometimes pick them up with two sticks to throw them out of reach of the sea, so that there would be one less danger for swimmers.

As a child I would stay at my great aunt's house at Hua Hin, a beach resort a half-day's drive from Bangkok, on the western shore of the Gulf of Thailand. As the daughter of a prince, it was almost obligatory that my great-aunt should have her holi-day house in Hua Hin which, since the Twenties, had been a second home for the Thai nobility. The region around Hua Hin had known royal visitors since the last century, but it was the construction of the railway link between the capital and Malaya, after the First World War, that put the sleepy seaside town within a four-hour train journey of Bangkok. In 1926 King Rama VII began work on his villa, Klai Kangwan, 'Far from worries', and this brought in its wake beach bungalows built by princes, princesses, and other court officials in the then fashionable style of English suburban bungalows. Visitors could stay at the Railway Hotel, a fairy-tale construction of wooden verandas with Victorian-style fret-work awnings, with topiary hedges carved into the shapes of animals apparently grazing on the well-watered lawns.

Prince Chula on holiday in Hua Hin in 1952

The king was to discover that 'Far from worries' was hardly the most appropriate name for his new residence for, in 1932, word came that there had been a revolution in Bangkok. Overnight His Majesty had been transformed from an absolute to a constitutional monarch. None of this affected Hua Hin which spent the next thirty years as a pleasant place for the well-to-do, away from any unrest in the capital. The town remained the country's principal resort until the Thai government started actively to promote tourism about twenty years ago. This led to the booming growth of Pattaya as the Miami Beach of South East Asia, a gaudy promenade of sky-scraper hotels, discos, massage parlours and international restaurants on the opposite side of the Gulf from sleepy old Hua Hin. The tourists have flocked to Pattaya. European ladies bare their breasts by the swimming pools, Arabs from the more

Page 100: Sun-dried fish, excellent for soup; hot and sour salad or with a spicy Nam Prik sauce

puritan parts of Islam come to enjoy the sins of the flesh, and every nationality can be found along its garish neon-lit main street, out for the evening stroll.

The more discriminating visitor has had to go further round the Gulf to enjoy the real pleasures of Thailand's coast, its wide deserted beaches and its simple fisher-folk life. Until ten years ago, those in the know made the journey to the island of Phuket, off the western side of the narrow isthmus that divides Thailand from Malaysia. Set in the Andaman Sea, the island offered simple accommodation in beach-side huts and the pleasures of freshly-caught fish and lobster grilled on an open fire. Nearby was Phangnga Bay, one of the world's most extraordinary natural beauty spots, a seascape dotted with surreal limestone outcrops; thin yet dizzyingly tall, rising dramatically out of the placid green waters. Built out into the bay on stilts, a fishing village offered wonderful food in a setting of breath-taking beauty. Too good to last, for in 1979 an international airport was opened and the hotels began to spring up. However, there is no need to despair, Thailand has many islands, and the adventurous can always keep one jump ahead of the builders. Today, young travellers backpack their way to the island of Koh Samui or continue down the coast from Pattaya to Koh Samet, a journey which takes them to the town of Rayong – famous as the main centre for the most essential ingredient in Thai food, fish sauce. There's no

Phangnga Bay, surrealist limestone outcrops rising from the sea. Now popular with tourists staying on the Island of Phuket

mistaking it, the whole place smells of drying fish. To offset the odour is the intriguing sight of thousands of pinkly translucent squid hung on lines to dry in the sun, like hosts of strange butterflies caught in gossamer nets.

While new resorts like Pattaya were springing up Hua Hin still remained largely unchanged. There was the addition of one or two more modern beach houses built by successful companies to provide weekend rest for their tired executives, but overall it was felt that the brasher aspects of the tourist trade should not infringe on the Royal Family's holiday home. A few miles to the north, at Cha'am, a modern hotel was built, but it is so neatly secluded from the old town that most of the tourists who stay there do not know that a short distance from where they are staying is a piece of fantasy well worth finding – near the local army barracks, right on the beach is a pleasure house built by King Rama VI, a series of airy wooden rooms on stilts, linked by walkways and verandas, one of which goes on out into the sea like an English pier. This was a place for parties and dalliance. Until recently, no one seemed to be responsible for looking after it and it was slowly crumbling away. It had the look of a haunted palace, a place of dreams, the only visitors an occasional group of young people who had ignored the warnings and clambered out onto the pavilion above the water to eat a picnic, play music, and laze an afternoon away. Happily, a decision has now been made to try to restore this magical place.

Today, Hua Hin's atmosphere of gentle decay may be ending. Faded scions of the older aristocracy still come for their holidays but the place has acquired a new smartness among the sophisticated young, who are drawn to its old-world charms. Change has been modest. The old Railway Hotel was spruced up with a coat of paint for its role as the Phnom Penh Hotel in the film *The Killing Fields*, and in 1986 the French Sofitel chain with their Thai partners undertook a sensitive restoration, keeping all the Thirties' fittings, so that the pleasures of the past have been improved by only the barest touches of modernity. My only complaint is that they have not kept the old name 'The Railway Hotel', with its nostalgic image of pre-war travel. However, as we Thais believe that your luck is improved if you walk under an elephant, so for me the best way to savour Hua Hin is still to enter the hotel by its gardens, passing under an enormous bush shaped like an elephant. In the foyer of the hotel one can admire a photograph of Miss Thailand 1940, and look into cabinets displaying the porcelain and silverware once used by the old Siamese Railways – worth more than a glance. After an aperitif you can ride in a *samloh* (a bicycle rickshaw) to the jetty, brightly flood-lit, where the larger motorized fishing boats have anchored. These are manned by tough deep-sea sailors, their arms blue with protective tattoos depicting religious or magical symbols. These wiry men live dangerously, often staying out for at least three days and nights at a time. The haul they bring is huge, a

*Unloading the catch
in Hua Hin harbour
at night*

tumbling avalanche of silvery fish destined for the shops and restaurants of Bangkok. At night, the scene is almost over-dramatic: weird figures wear cloth hoods with eye-holes, like Halloween ghosts, to protect their skin from the sharp fish scales; ships about to depart are loaded with crushed ice which steams in the hot air adding to the aura of mystery. After the best of the catch has been tossed from hand to hand, from boat to truck, the tiny sprats and the sweepings are loaded into baskets destined for the duck farms that supply Bangkok's insatiable appetite for that delicious bird.

Having admired the haul, it is time to sample it. There is a fish-market at the entrance to the jetty and beside that, a row of restaurants. It is to one of these wooden rooms, jutting out on stilts over the water, that the visitor must go for an evening meal. At the entrance is a brightly lit stall groaning under the results of the owner's bargaining session with the fishermen: a cascade of glistening clams, white and purple squid, a tank crowded with so many fish only the fisherfolk know their names. But the diners will have no problem choosing their meal, a young helper will offer a book of photographs illustrating the cook's specialities. She can be seen just behind the stall waiting near her wok for the choice of ingredients to be made. A fish is pointed out, the net dips into the tank; mussels are selected, a handful are scooped up – all go into the wok so fast you can barely follow her movements. It is all as easy and as abundant as the seas and rivers of Thailand itself which teem with fish so that the smallest child can be sure of a catch. If Bangkok floods in the rainy season, shoals of fish migrate up the city's highways, darting and weaving about the half-submerged cars as if they were so may rocks.

After the main meal, diners can stroll from the restaurant to the Hua Hin market in the centre of town where night-time food stalls are set out with tropical fruit, sweetmeats and

*Previous pages:
Fishing boats
riding at anchor off
Hua Hin*

puddings, ice creams and cold drinks to finish off the evening's dining. If you are lucky enough to be staying in a beach bungalow you can return via the moonlit sands where the final pleasure is to watch the lights flickering on the boats of the in-shore fishermen waiting for the night's catch to enter their long line of nets. In the morning these shallow-bottomed boats will be dragged as near the shore as possible offering the

*Fishing by night in
the Gulf of Thailand*

haul to the occupants of the holiday homes. Crabs will be
bought by the bucketful for a great steamed feast. There will be
lobsters and prawns, floundering and scrabbling about in the
bottom of the vessel. But at night these boats are merely dark
shapes gently tossed on the returning tide while on the nearby
headland a giant statue of the Buddha silently watches over the
waters offering protection to all those who live by the sea.

PREPARATION OF FISH & SEAFOOD

Wholesale fish market at the harbour entrance, Hua Hin

Any fishmonger will gut, clean and scale a fish at your request and it is obviously much easier to ask for this to be done rather than undertake the task yourself. But if you do so, slit the underside of the fish from under and behind the head to the lower fin; remove the innards; wash the cavity under cold running water. Scale, if necessary, with a knife, scraping from tail to head. You may wish the head to remain: so cut off the gills and trim the fins with scissors. Wash the fish thoroughly under cold running water and pat dry inside and out before cooking.

Mussels, clams and oysters can be rinsed under running water. Mussels should be de-bearded. Oyster shells, sometimes muddy in the crevices, can be lightly scrubbed. The amount of sand and grit within the shell of clams and mussels may be such that they will need to be soaked for some time before cooking. Ask your fishmonger as some types can be bought quite clean and need only a cursory rinsing. Any mussels or clams which, before cooking, do not close when given a good shaking together, discard. Similarly, discard any which remain closed after cooking.

Crabs, lobsters and other spiny seafood, if bought live, may be killed by plunging into a large pan of already boiling well-salted water for 15-20 minutes, depending on size, until the shell turns bright red. Some people feel it more humane to place the creatures into cold salted water and then bring slowly to the boil; they will become slowly unconscious as the temperature increases. To open a cooked lobster, turn the beast on its back, insert the point of a stout knife between body and tail, and split first the tail, then the body. Remove the black thread of intestine from the tail (devein), and remove the small sac of sand and grit in the head. You can eat everything else. Crack the claws to remove the meat.

The recipes in this book need ready-prepared crabmeat which is easily available in fishmongers along with their shells.

Large prawns (king prawns) – often tails only – can be bought fresh or frozen. They should be deveined before cooking by shelling and cutting along the back and removing the black thread-like intestine. The whole prawns can be bought already-cooked, and can be further grilled, and the head and shell removed at table.

Smaller prawns (American shrimp) are sold fresh or frozen, and have usually been cooked at sea. They have also usually already been beheaded and shelled, but can sometimes be bought whole with head and tail.

Some shrimp are small enough to eat whole, particularly some species available in our waters, but you might prefer to remove the head from the slightly larger ones.

Squid are available in various sizes, the bodies ranging from about 3-10 in/7.5-25cm, or even longer. They can be bought already cleaned and ready for cooking, but these will be body sacs only. If you buy squid fresh and whole, they should be prepared as follows:

1. Pull the tentacled head and innards from the body sac. Cut off the tentacles and reserve; discard the head and attached innards.

2. Inside the sac is a long transparent piece of cartilage, the backbone, 'pen' or 'quill'. Remove by pulling it gently away while washing the sac under water.

3. The sac is covered by a very thin pinkish-brown mottled fine skin which is easily pulled away leaving the sac flesh milky white. The two fins may be left on.

Opposite: Hot and sour Seafood Salad

TYPES OF FISH

The waters in and around Thailand provide an amazing variety of fish. But not all are available in the West though some are now imported frozen, so the following recipes use fish more readily available in European and American markets.

For grilling (broiling) almost any fish is suitable, from the magnificent (and expensive) sea bass to the modest herring. Steaming is a good method for the more fragrant-fleshed fish such as bass, turbot or trout (though I find our own pomfret is a good 'all-rounder'). Small flat fish are suitable for deep frying, eg. plaice or pomfret, as are round fish such as whiting or grey mullet; but it would be nothing less than a crime to fry the fragrant flesh of the sea bass or turbot. The following is a much less than comprehensive list of fish which can be used in Thai cooking:

Sea bass	Codling (small cod)
Flounder	Herring
Mackerel	Grey Mullet
Red Mullet	Perch
Plaice	Pomfret
Sardine	Snapper
Sole (Lemon/Dover)	Trout
Turbot	Whitebait
Whiting	

When selecting from this list, remember size and price, and that the 'oily' fish (herring, mackerel, sardine) have a fairly strong flavour and need strong sauces.

For recipes requiring fillets or steaks, those from the larger fish can also be used such as cod, coley, haddock, hake, halibut, etc. as well as the flesh of the monk- or angler-fish. And of course, fillets or steaks may also be steamed, grilled or fried.

BARBECUED SEAFOOD
Talay Thai

This is the most elementary Thai seafood dish, the sort of thing a family would prepare on a day's outing: they would buy a basket of mixed fish (squid, prawns, etc.), in a seaside market and then have a barbecue. While this method of cooking produces the best flavour, grilling/broiling is an obvious substitute. For this recipe I have chosen squid, but prawns, lobster or any firm fresh fish will do for this dish.

2 large squid (bodies about 6-9in/15-23cm long), cleaned, sac and tentacles separated
Sauce:
3 tbs/45ml lemon juice
2 large garlic cloves, finely chopped
2 small green chillies, finely chopped
2 tsp/10ml sugar

Pre-heat the barbecue or grill/broiler. Cut each squid body sac lengthways into quarters, ensuring that the interior surfaces are clean. With a sharp knife lightly score both sides of each piece diagonally, into a diamond pattern (this will help the cooking process and make the final dish more attractive). Leave the tentacled heads whole for grilling – they can be cut up after cooking. Lay all the squid pieces on the grill and cook for about 10 minutes on each side until they are well browned: the body pieces should curl up.

While the squid is cooking, put the fish sauce, lemon juice, chopped garlic, chillis and sugar in a small bowl. Stir well to combine. Arrange the cooked squid on a large dish and put the sauce in its bowl in the middle. The squid pieces should be dipped into the sauce and eaten with the fingers.

Pomfret, now available in the West

A dried fish stall: hard sun-dried prawns and crispy wafers of squid

GRILLED FISH WITH CORIANDER AND GARLIC

Pla Pow

This is one of the simplest fish dishes. At home we wrap the fish in banana leaves and cook it on an open charcoal fire. Some Chinese supermarkets do stock banana leaves, so this method might be possible, but you can also use aluminium foil instead, and use your ordinary grill/broiler. Serve this with the sauce that accompanies Barbecued Seafood, (p. 112).

6 coriander roots
3 large garlic cloves
ground white pepper
1 mackerel or whiting, cleaned and patted dry inside and out
lettuce leaves, to garnish

Pre-heat the barbecue or grill/broiler.

With a pestle and mortar or blender, pound or grind the coriander roots and garlic together to form a paste and mix in a generous shaking of ground white pepper. Put this paste in the cavity of the cleaned fish. Wrap the fish in a banana leaf or foil; if using a banana leaf, simply roll the wide leaf around the stuffed fish, fold the ends over and secure the package with toothpicks. Grill/broil the fish for about 6-8 minutes each side. To serve, simply unwrap the fish and place on a bed of lettuce.

STEAMED FISH WITH GINGER AND MUSHROOMS

Pla Nung King

1 pomfret or similar fish, cleaned, and scored 2-3 times on each side
1 abalone (oyster) mushroom, or fresh field mushroom, finely sliced
1½in/4cm piece ginger, cut into matchstick pieces
2in/5cm piece pickled cabbage (Pak Gat Dong) or 3-4 pieces of pickled red cabbage, slivered lengthways
2in/5cm fresh red chilli, slivered lengthways
2 spring onions/scallions, finely sliced into 2in/5cm pieces
2 tbs/30ml fish sauce
1 tbs/15ml light soy sauce
½ tsp/2.5ml ground white pepper
1 tbs/15ml whisky (optional)
coriander leaves, to garnish

Put the prepared fish on a dish slightly larger than itself, which will fit into your steamer, or into a large saucepan with an inverted saucer or small bowl in the bottom of it. Place all the remaining ingredients, except the garnish on top of the fish. Put the dish in the steamer and steam for 20-25 minutes. Remove, garnish with the coriander and serve.

FRIED FISH WITH PORK, GINGER AND MUSHROOMS

Pla Jian

This is another simple dish and quite mild in flavour.

oil for deep frying, plus 2 tbs/30ml
1 pomfret or other small flat fish, cleaned, rinsed, and patted dry inside and out
2 garlic cloves, finely chopped
3oz/90g minced/ground pork
1 small carrot, cut diagonally into 4-5 pieces
1in/2.5cm piece ginger, finely slivered
4-6 pieces Thai dried black mushroom, soaked in water for about 15 minutes to soften
1 tsp/5ml yellow bean sauce
1 tbs/15ml light soy sauce
1 tbs/15ml fish sauce
1 tsp/5ml sugar
4 tbs/60 ml stock/broth
½ small onion, slivered
1 medium red chilli, finely slivered
2 spring onions/scallions, trimmed and coarsely chopped
generous shake of ground white pepper

Heat the oil and deep-fry the fish until golden brown and crisp. Remove, drain, place on a serving dish and set aside. While the fish is cooking, heat 2 tbs/30ml of oil in a wok or frying pan/skillet. Add the garlic and fry until golden brown. Add the pork, stir and cook until the meat is no longer pink. Add the remaining ingredients, one at a time, stirring and cooking for a second or two after each addition. Turn the mixture onto the cooked fish and serve.

THREE-FLAVOURED FISH

Pla Lat Prik

This dish typifies Thai cooking: it combines three opposing flavours – sweet, sour and hot – yet allows each to remain distinct and separate. This recipe also works well with sea bass but this is, unfortunately, extremely expensive. However, if you prefer to make this recipe with bass, buy a medium-sized fish and grill/broil rather than fry it.

1 mackerel or whiting (about 1 lb/450g), cleaned and gutted with head left on
oil for deep frying
lettuce, to garnish

Sauce:
2 tbs/30ml oil
6 shallots, finely chopped
1 large garlic clove, finely chopped
4 red chillies, 3in/7.5cm long, deseeded and finely chopped
2 tbs/30ml fish sauce
2 tbs/30ml sugar
2 tbs/30ml lemon juice
2 tbs/30ml stock

Fill a frying pan large enough to hold the fish with oil to a depth of 1 in/2.5cm. Heat the oil until a light haze appears. Add the fish and fry until the skin (and some of the flesh) is crisp and golden on both sides, making sure it doesn't stick to the pan.

While the fish is cooking, make the sauce. In a small frying pan heat 2 tbs/30ml oil and fry the shallots until crisp and brown, then remove with a slotted spoon and set aside. Fry the garlic until golden brown, remove with a slotted spoon, and set aside. Pour off most of the oil from the pan leaving a light film. Return half the cooked shallots and garlic to the pan and add the chillies, fish sauce, sugar, lemon juice and stock. Stir until the sugar is dissolved and the mixture starts to thicken slightly. Add the remaining shallots and garlic, stir and remove from heat.

Arrange the lettuce on a serving dish. When the fish is cooked, remove from the pan and place on the bed of lettuce. Pour the sauce over and serve.

Above: Sun-drying squid at Rayong. Left: Opening giant Thai oysters

BABY CLAMS IN BATTER WITH EGG AND CHILLI

Hoy Tohd

Batter:
3 tbs/45ml rice flour

3 tbs/45ml wheat flour

2 eggs

pinch of salt

8fl oz/240ml/1 cup water

1½lbs baby clams, shelled
(should yield 4-6oz/120-180g meat)

3 tbs/45ml oil, plus extra if necessary

1 garlic clove, finely chopped

ground white pepper

1 tbs/15ml light soy sauce

2 tbs/30ml fish sauce

1 tsp/5ml sugar

handful beansprouts

1 spring onion/scallion, coarsely chopped

coriander leaf for garnish

Sauce:
3 tbs/45ml rice vinegar

2 small chillies, sliced into fine rings

½ tsp/2.5ml sugar

Put the flours in a basin and mix thoroughly with the pinch of salt. Break one egg into the flour mixture, mix, add the water. Whisk thoroughly together, making sure there are no lumps; the mixture should have the consistency of thick cream. Add the shelled clams and set aside.

In a large frying pan/skillet, heat the oil and fry the garlic until golden. Add the clam and batter mixture, tipping the pan to spread it evenly over the surface to form a pancake. Turn after 1-2 minutes (it will cook quickly), and cook the other side briefly. With a spatula and wooden spoon, or similar instruments, quickly tear the clam pancake into five or six pieces. Lower the heat and break the second egg into the pan. Quickly cook the pancake pieces in the egg. Add a little more oil if necessary, and then a sprinkling of white pepper, the soy sauce, fish sauce and sugar, turning the pancake pieces quickly as you work. Add the beansprouts and spring onion and turn together quickly. Turn the mixture onto a heated dish and garnish with coriander. In a small bowl, blend the vinegar, chillies and sugar and serve with the clam cake.

Hauling in the nets at dusk on Lamai beach on the island of Koh Samui

HOT AND SOUR SEAFOOD SALAD
Yam Talay

This is only for lovers of chilli. It has a very sharp, lemony taste and is often served as a pre-meal starter with drinks: its electric flavour is said to sober up those who've had one too many. It can be made with any combination of seafood.

lettuce, parsley, cucumber, etc. to garnish
2 tbs/30ml lemon juice
1 tsp/5ml chilli powder
2 tbs/30ml stock/broth
1 tsp/5ml sugar
2 tbs/30ml fish sauce
4 prepared fish balls (from an oriental store)
4 large raw prawns, shelled and deveined
2-4 crab claws
4 pieces sliced squid
2 lime leaves, finely sliced
1 shallot, finely chopped
½ small onion, finely slivered
sprig of coriander leaf, coarsely chopped

Prepare a serving dish with lettuce, parsley and sliced cucumber and set aside. Combine the lemon juice, chilli powder, stock, sugar and fish sauce in a small pan. Bring to the boil, stirring all the time. Add the fish balls, prawns, crab claws and squid, and stir and cook for a minute or two until the raw meats are cooked through. Take off the heat and add all the remaining ingredients. Mix well, turn onto the prepared dish, and serve.

PRAWNS WITH LEMON GRASS
Pla Gung

lettuce and parsley sprigs, to decorate
2 tbs/30ml lemon juice
2 tbs/30ml fish sauce
½ tsp/2.5ml chilli powder
1 tsp/5ml sugar
2 tbs/30ml stock/broth
4-6 large prawns, shelled and deveined
1 lime leaf, finely sliced
1 shallot, coarsely chopped
⅓ lemon grass stalk, finely chopped
½ small onion, slivered
1 spring onion/scallion, cut into 1in/2.5cm pieces

Prepare a small serving plate with lettuce and sprigs of parsley.

Boil the lemon juice with the fish sauce, chilli powder, sugar and stock for about a minute in a small pan, over high heat, stirring. Add the shelled prawns and cook quickly until the prawns are opaque. The liquid should be considerably reduced. Add the remaining ingredients, stir once, remove from the heat and transfer immediately to the prepared plate.

BATTERED PRAWNS WITH FRESH PICKLES
Tod Man Gung

The pleasure of this dish is the contrast between the bland batter and the sharp taste of the vegetables in vinegar. It can be eaten as a snack or starter.

oil for frying
lettuce, to garnish
Batter:
4oz/120g rice flour
1oz/30g dessicated coconut
1 egg
8fl oz/250ml/1cup water
½ tsp/5ml salt
6oz/180g small prawns (if using frozen, ensure they are properly defrosted) or small shrimp
Sauce:
4 tbs/60ml rice or other white vinegar
1 tbs/15ml sugar
2 small red chillies, chopped into fine rings
1 tbs/15ml ground peanuts
2 shallots, chopped
1½in/4cm piece cucumber, quartered lengthways, then finely sliced
1 spring onion/scallion, chopped
1 small sprig of coriander leaf, chopped

Make the batter. Measure the rice flour and coconut into a bowl and stir together. Break in the egg and blend. Using a whisk, stir the water into the mixture making sure it is smooth and without lumps: it should be the consistency of very thick cream. Add the salt, mix, and set aside.

Make the sauce. Boil the rice vinegar and sugar together until the sugar dissolves. Set aside to cool. When cool, pour into a small bowl, add the rest of the sauce ingredients and mix well.

Line a serving dish with lettuce. Pour 1½ in/4cm depth of oil into a frying pan and heat. Mix the prawns into the batter, making sure that each prawn is thoroughly coated. When the oil is hot, gradually spoon half the prawn mixture into the pan and, by keeping all the prawns together, shape into a cake, adding a little extra batter to the 'cake', if necessary, to make sure it holds together. Fry on both sides until golden brown and crisp. This will only take a minute or two. Remove the prawn 'cake' from the oil and drain on kitchen paper. Repeat the process with the remaining battered prawns. Serve both prawn cakes on a bed of lettuce with the sour and sweet sauce on the side.

PRAWNS WITH GINGER
Gung Siam

2 tbs/30ml oil
2 garlic cloves, finely chopped
1in/2.5cm piece ginger, finely sliced
6-8 large prawns, peeled and deveined
¼ tsp/1.25ml ground white pepper
1 tbs/15ml light soy sauce
2 tbs/30ml fish sauce
½ tsp/2.5ml sugar
2 tbs/30ml stock/broth or water
2 spring onions/scallions cut into 2in/5cm slices
1 small onion, sliced

In a wok or frying pan, heat the oil until a light haze appears. Add the garlic and fry until golden brown. Add the ginger and stir. Add the prawns, stir thoroughly, then add the pepper, soy sauce, fish sauce, sugar and stock or water. Stirring continually, cook until the prawns are opaque and cooked through – about 2 minutes. Add the sliced spring onions and onion, stir once, remove from the heat and serve.

Roes, sun-dried inside whole fish

A stall-holder sprinkles water on a fresh catch

PRAWN CURRY
Gangkuwa Gung

This has a thick, rich and creamy taste and the final bright red colour is very appealing.

2 tbs/30ml oil
1 large garlic clove, finely chopped
1 tbs/15ml Red curry paste (p.93)
8fl oz/250ml/1cup coconut milk
2 tbs/30ml fish sauce
1 tsp/5ml sugar
12 large raw prawns, about 3in/7.5cm long, deveined, beheaded and peeled, but with the small tail shell left on
2 lime leaves, finely sliced
1 small red chilli, finely sliced lengthwise
10 leaves holy basil

In a wok or frying pan, heat the oil, add the chopped garlic and fry until golden brown. Add the curry paste, stir with the garlic and cook briefly. Stirring briskly after each addition, add half the coconut milk, the fish sauce and the sugar. The mixture will thicken slightly. Add the prawns and cook until they start to become opaque. Add the remaining half of the coconut milk, the lime leaves and the chilli. Continue to cook, turning the prawns in the sauce until they are cooked through. With a slotted spoon or tongs, re-

Previous pages: Thai seafood. Clockwise: Three-flavoured fish; baby clams with black bean sauce; squid with vegetables and oyster sauce; steamed mussels with lemon grass and basil; barbecued prawns with hot sauce

move the prawns from the sauce and arrange them on a serving dish. Add the basil leaves to the sauce, stir, pour the sauce over the prawns and serve.

FRIED CRAB CLAWS WITH CURRY POWDER
Bu Pad Pung Karee

Despite its name, this is not an especially 'hot' dish. The curry powder is used to add flavour, not heat, rather in the way Western cooks use Eastern spices, also without their usual chilli heat.

lettuce leaves, to garnish
2 tbs/15ml oil
1 large garlic clove, finely chopped
4-6 crab claws, depending on size
2 tbs/30ml stock/broth
1 tsp/5ml curry powder
1 tbs/15ml light soy sauce
½ tsp/2.5ml sugar
2 tbs/30ml fish sauce
1 small onion, slivered
2 spring onions/scallions, coarsely chopped
6-8 pieces of finely sliced sweet red pepper
coriander leaves, to garnish

Line a serving dish with lettuce leaves. In a wok or frying pan/skillet, heat the oil, add the garlic and fry until golden brown. Add the crab claws and stir quickly, then add the remaining ingredients, one by one (except the coriander leaves), stirring and cooking for a few seconds after each addition. Turn onto the prepared serving dish and garnish with the coriander leaves.

STEAMED CRAB MEAT
Bu Ja

The first time you make this recipe you will need to buy 4 crab shells as well as the meat, the next time you can just buy the crab meat. If crab shells are unavailable, use heatproof ramekins instead.

3 garlic cloves
3 coriander roots
4oz/120g crabmeat
4oz/120g minced/ground pork
1 egg
2 tbs/30ml fish sauce
1 tbs/15ml light soy sauce
½ tsp/2.5ml sugar
4 crab shells
Garnish:
8 fine slivers red chilli (or red pepper)
8 fine slivers green chilli (or green pepper)
8 coriander leaves

Pound the garlic with the coriander roots. Mix all the ingredients, except the garnishes, thoroughly together. Put the mixture into the crab shells (or ramekins) and arrange in a steamer. Steam for 15 minutes. Remove and garnish with the slivers of green and red chilli and coriander leaves.

STEAMED CRAB CLAWS
Bu Op

This dish is traditionally cooked in a clay pot which can be bought in most Chinese or oriental stores.

2 tbs/30ml oil
2 garlic cloves, finely chopped
3oz/90g dry *Wun Sen* noodles (p. 86), soaked for 15 minutes in cold water and drained
1in/2.5cm piece ginger, cut into matchstick strips
2 celery stalks/sticks, sliced diagonally
2oz/60g broccoli florets
2oz/60g spring greens/cabbage, coarsely chopped
4-6 crab claws, depending on size
1 tsp/5ml dark soy sauce
1 tbs/15ml light soy sauce
½ tsp/2.5ml sugar
2 tbs/30ml fish sauce
1 tbs/15ml oyster sauce
2 tbs/30ml stock/broth or water

In a wok or large frying pan, heat the oil, add the garlic and fry until golden brown. Add the vermicelli, stir quickly, then add the ginger, celery, broccoli and cabbage and stir briefly. Add the crab claws and stir. Add all the remaining ingredients, stir quickly, cover and steam gently for 3-4 minutes. If you think the mixture is becoming too dry, add a little more stock or water.

SQUID WITH VEGETABLES AND OYSTER SAUCE
Plamuk Patpak Namanhoy

This is another variation of a basic Thai theme: meat or fish plus crisp fresh vegetables. In this case it's squid with whatever seasonal vegetables are available; I have suggested ingredients that look good (a very Thai way of approaching food), but the really important thing is to use whatever vegetables are freshest when you shop.

6oz/180g squid (bodies only), rinsed and drained if bought ready prepared
2 tbs/30ml oil
2 garlic cloves, finely chopped
1 tbs/15ml oyster sauce
4-5 small baby corn, each cut lengthwise into 2-3 pieces
2 tbs/30ml fish sauce
1 tbs/15ml light soy sauce
½ tsp/2.5ml sugar
1 large red chilli, sliced into rings about 2 tbs/30 ml water
4-5 pieces dried mushroom, soaked in water for 15 minutes and sliced if necessary
10 stalks Thai spring flower (available from specialist stores) or 2 spring onions/scallions, cut into 1½-2in/4-5cm pieces
5-6 mangetout/snow peas, trimmed
5-6 small broccoli florets

Slice the squid bodies into rings and set aside. In a wok or large frying pan, heat the oil, add the garlic and fry until golden brown. Add the oyster sauce and baby corn and stir. Then add the squid, stir and cook for a few seconds. Add the remaining ingredients, one at a time, stirring after each addition. Cook briefly until the broccoli is a good bright green and still crisp, and the squid is cooked through, opaque, and slightly shrunken. If you feel the mixture is becoming too dry, add a little more water.

SQUID WITH DRY CURRY
Plamuk Patpet

This dish is hot. Its appeal lies in the contrast between the bland squid and green aubergines/eggplant, and the fiery attack of the red chillies.

6-8oz/180-230g squid (bodies only), washed and cleaned
3 tbs/45ml oil
2 garlic cloves, finely chopped
2 tsp/10ml Red curry paste (p. 93)
2 tbs/30ml fish sauce
1 tbs/15ml light soy sauce
1 tsp/5ml sugar
2-3 small green aubergine/eggplant, quartered, or Western aubergine
1 small red chilli, finely chopped
2 lime leaves, finely sliced
10 leaves holy basil

Score the squid quite finely on both sides, and cut into pieces, about 1 in/2.5cm square. In a wok or frying pan, over medium-high flame, heat the oil, add the garlic and fry until golden brown. Add the curry paste, mix, and cook for a few seconds. Now add the squid, mix and cook briefly. Stirring all the time, add the remaining ingredients, pausing after the addition of the aubergines to give them a few seconds to cook. When the squid is cooked through and opaque, give a final stir, pour the mixture onto a warmed dish and serve.

Sorting fresh green-tinged mussels, like the oysters, much larger than in the West

STUFFED SQUID SOUP
Gang Juhd Pla Muk Yat Sai

4oz/120g minced/ground pork
2 garlic cloves, finely chopped
½ tsp/2.5ml ground white pepper
1 tbs/15ml fish sauce
½ tsp/2.5 ml sugar
5-6 small squid body sacs (3-4in/8-10cm long)
1pt/570ml stock/broth
2 tbs/30ml fish sauce
2 tbs/30ml light soy sauce
1 tsp/5ml preserved radish (*tang chi*, p. 39)
½ tsp/2.5ml ground white pepper
2 spring onions/scallions, cut into 1in/2.5cm pieces

Thoroughly combine the pork, garlic, white pepper, 1 tbs fish sauce and sugar. Stuff the mixture into the squid sacs, taking care not to overfill them since the filling will swell in cooking. In a medium-sized pan, heat the stock and add 2 tbs fish sauce, soy sauce, preserved radish, and pepper. When thoroughly blended and heated through, bring to a simmer, add the stuffed squid and cook gently for 4-5 minutes. The squid will shrink and the meat mixture cook through. Add the sliced spring onions and serve in small bowls.

STEAMED MUSSELS WITH LEMON GRASS & BASIL
Hoy Op

Those used to cooking mussels with cream and wine will be pleasantly surprised by the simplicity of this Thai recipe. Galangal, lemon grass and holy basil all delicately enhance the mussel flavour.

1-1½lb/450-700g mussels, cleaned, debearded, and rinsed
3in/8cm piece galangal, in 3-4 pieces
2 lemon grass stalks, cut into 3in/8cm pieces and lightly crushed
10 sprigs holy basil
Sauce:
1 large garlic clove, finely chopped
1 tsp/5ml chopped chilli
2 tbs/30ml lemon juice
1 tbs/15ml light soy sauce
2 tbs/30ml fish sauce
1 tsp/5ml sugar

Place the mussels, galangal, lemon grass and basil in a large saucepan. Add enough water to come ½ in/1cm up the pan. Cover, place over medium heat and steam for about 15 minutes or until the mussels have opened. Discard any mussels that do not open.

Combine the sauce ingredients in a small bowl. Serve the mussels in a large bowl, with the sauce nearby for dipping the mussels into.

BABY CLAMS WITH BLACK BEAN SAUCE
Hoy Pat Tow Jeow

This dish is best made with small sweet clams, rather than with the big clams that are most usual in North American cooking.

2 tbs/30ml oil
2 garlic cloves, finely chopped
1 lb/450g baby clams in the shell
2 tbs/30ml light soy sauce
1 small red chilli, finely chopped
1 tsp/5ml black bean sauce
4 tbs/60ml water
10 leaves holy basil

In a wok or large frying pan, heat the oil, add the garlic and fry until golden brown. Add the baby clams and stir thoroughly. Add the soy sauce, chilli, black bean sauce, and the water. Stir thoroughly, add the basil, cover the pan and leave to steam for a few minutes until the clams have opened. Discard any that have not opened. Stir again, turn onto a warmed dish and serve.

STEAMED SCALLOPS WITH GARLIC
Hoy Nung Kratiem Jeow

A delicate starter, easy to make, but very luxurious.

6 scallops on the shell, cleaned
3 tbs/45ml oil
3 garlic cloves, finely chopped
1 small red or green chilli, sliced into fine rings
Sauce:
3 tbs/45ml light soy sauce
1in/2.5cm piece ginger, finely chopped
1 tsp/5ml sugar
1 small red chilli, finely chopped
Garnish:
2 tbs/30ml spring onion/scallion, sliced into fine rings
6 coriander leaves

Set the scallops on their shells in a steamer over 1-2 in/2.5-5cm hot water. In a small frying pan, heat the oil, add the garlic and fry until golden brown. Pour a spoonful of garlic and oil over each scallop, add a little sliced chilli, cover, and steam over medium heat until the scallops are cooked (10-15 minutes). While the scallops steam, mix together all the sauce ingredients.

When the scallops are cooked, remove from the steamer, place on a serving dish and garnish with the spring onion and coriander leaves. Serve the sauce on the side.

CRAB OMELETTE
Kai Jeow Poo

3oz/90g white crabmeat
1 tsp/5ml sesame oil
1 tbs/15ml white wine
3 eggs
2 tbs/15ml coconut cream
½ tsp/2.5ml salt
shaking of ground white pepper
1 tbs/15ml finely slivered ginger
1 tbs/15ml finely slivered carrot
1 tbs/15ml finely slivered onion
1 tbs/15ml finely slivered bamboo shoot
1 tbs/15ml finely sliced straw mushrooms
2 tbs/30ml oil
coriander leaves, to garnish

Combine the crabmeat, sesame oil and white wine in a small bowl and set aside. In a bowl, lightly beat the eggs with the coconut cream, salt and pepper. Add the crab mixture and blend lightly. Add the ginger, carrot, onion, bamboo shoot and mushrooms. Lightly mix together.

In a wok or frying pan, heat the oil until a light haze appears. Pour the mixture into the oil. With a spatula, gently lift the egg from the sides of the wok as it cooks to allow the uncooked mixture to set. Turn it over, and cook for a few seconds. When the omelette is set, slide it onto a serving dish and garnish with coriander leaves.

UP COUNTRY

FOOD FROM THE NORTHERN REGIONS
OF THAILAND

s the morning mist clears across a heavily wooded valley a young man is picking wild mushrooms by a stream, laying them carefully in a chipped enamel bowl. These mushrooms are quite unlike the neat button variety eaten in Europe. They look more like undulant sea creatures the colour of old ivory. These meaty fungi will provide a tasty part of the morning meal and they are free, which is no bad thing. Walking back to his hamlet, the man seems, at a distance, to be passing through untamed forest but close-to can be seen patches of cultivation between the trees where rice and vegetables are growing. These are the foothills of the mountain range that rises into the Golden Triangle, the high northern region that Thailand shares with Burma and Laos. Beyond this valley live the hill tribes who are racially different from the lowland Thai. In the extreme northern highlands, these tribes are often a law unto themselves. Locked in their mountain strongholds War Lords control the opium trade, slipping across the frontiers to escape the Thai army.

King Rama VII entering Chiang Mai on an elephant, 1927

But all that is far away. Here, safe beside the regional capital, Chiang Mai, a new day breaks clear at Wat Chet Yot unveiling the ancient carvings on its tall square Chedi. Even a short-term visitor coming from Bangkok will see that this temple is different in style from those in the south. The Chedi, with its seven spires, is decorated with bas-relief figures, princely in appearance, whose elegant limbs are turned as if in some formal dance, their lips frozen in serene smiles. The design of this temple, like many in the north has been heavily influenced by neighbouring Burma. Wat Chet Yot is one of the most famous centres in Buddhist history as it was here, in 1477, that the king of then independent Chiang Mai, Tilokaraje, summoned a great Council from all over Asia to revise the sacred teachings of the Buddha. The temple itself is a copy of that in Pagan, Burma, which itself was copied from that in Bodh Gaya, India where the Buddha achieved enlightenment. Inside the vaulted prayer-hall the huge wooden Buddha has the almost doll-like simplicity that we associate with Burmese folk art, a distinct contrast to the refined carvings on the outside walls. The temple tells us much about the north and its remoteness from the centre of Thai culture. The influence of Burma has filtered into the art, the customs, and of course the food of Chiang Mai. This northern city is the Bankokians favourite escape from the hot season humidity of the capital and whereas the southerners delight in telling rude jokes about the ignorance of provincials, especially the peoples of the

Page 124: A Burmese-style temple nestling in the foot-hills of Northern Thailand

north east whose accent is considered amusing, they have nothing but praise for the citizens of Chiang Mai, who are said to
be more polite, more generous and helpful. They also say that
the girls of Chiang Mai are the prettiest in the country and that
the region's food is the tastiest.

Some years back, my aunt and uncle bought part of Mae Sae
valley, in the hills to the north west of the town, and created a
garden resort with pleasant flowerbeds on slopes running
down to a river at the valley bottom. Among these plants and
shrubs are thatched cottages where tired city folk can spend a
relaxing weekend. Like me, my aunt was a student in Britain
and is passionate about the English garden so that foreign
visitors are sometimes puzzled when they find themselves ad-
miring well-tended borders of geraniums, or whatever bulbs

*Ancient stucco on
the wall of Wat Chet
Yot on the outskirts
of Chiang Mai*

Mr Gee and his family enjoy a meal they have grown and cooked themselves

she has brought back from her holidays or that I have been prevailed upon to send her. And not just flowers, my aunt experiments with all sorts of temperate plants and her kitchen gardens now supply the big Bangkok hotels with rare Italian salads and French vegetables. Of course, this is all part of an honourable Thai tradition of drawing new elements into our cuisine – the Portuguese introduced the chilli which they brought from the Americas in the seventeenth century, and more recently we have added the tomato, the potato, carrots, celery and sweet peppers. It is a living tradition. The formal English garden is much admired by the Thai, who greatly envy the open spaces of English cities. At Mae Sae valley there is a chance to enjoy that pleasure in the cool clear highland air. Today, most visitors fly up but for the full effect you should take the old fashioned train which chugs its way overnight up the length of the country, crossing the wide rice paddies of the central plains and passing on to the vast teak forests of the north.

In among those forests, near my family's resort, the traditional life of the north goes on. Returning with his bowl of mushrooms, our young man greets his father-in-law at work in his patch of rice. They cultivate sticky, or glutinous rice, the staple food of the region. Sticky rice is only a novelty in the rest of the world, and even in Bangkok we seldom eat it except as a dessert, so it has little export value and the farmers here are less well-off than those in the south. Nevertheless, the cool climate provides compensations with abundant harvests of vegetables that can be sold elsewhere, and temperate crops such as apples, grapes and strawberries that cannot be grown in the heat of the lowland plains.

The young man has moved in with his wife's family. His father-in-law, Mr Gee, has partially retired, leaving most of the cultivation to the younger members of the family. They all live in a compound of stilt houses, the interiors are rich dark teak polished by the rubbing of bare feet. The only possessions in the old man's room are a few mats and a radio, from which comes a further episode in that gripping daily soap opera: "He has deceived her after all. On reaching the city she has discovered that he already has two wives but there is no going back . . ." Mrs Gee gives her youngest grand-daughter a meaningful stare. Underneath the houses are bulbous pottery rain jars and a stack of fresh buffalo dung that will be used to line the wicker rice store. Stray dogs and chickens scavenge in the shade. Across the compound is the communal kitchen with a charcoal brazier and heavy stone mortar. Before the gate of the compound is a water-jar with a ladle made of half a coconut, in case any passer-by should need refreshment; hospitality is a strong tradition here.

Although over eighty, Mr Gee is fit and lean from years of healthy labour. His father settled this land when it was unoccupied wild country, available to whoever could farm it. He has no title deeds and for most of his life has lived outside the reach of the administration, knowing little of the cash economy. He would hire out his labour for one or two days a year to earn the few coins needed to buy the odd items of equipment and dress that could not be made in the village. In those far-off days, he and a group of friends would walk over the mountain tracks to Chiang Mai to make purchases for the entire community. What today is a half-hour car journey took them eight hours of difficult jungle trekking, with snakes and even tigers to contend with. He made that journey one unforgettable day in 1927 when King Rama VII and Queen Rambaibani became the first Thai monarchs to take possession of their northern capital, riding into Chiang Mai at the head of a procession of eighty-four brightly caparisoned elephants.

The city had until then been left in the hands of a family of hereditary Governor-Princes, vassals of the 'Lord of Life' in faraway Krung Thep.

For centuries Chiang Mai had been capital of an independent kingdom but the interminable wars with Burma eventually destroyed it. But even in the eighteenth century, when the north was absorbed into Siam by the new Chakri dynasty in Bangkok, little changed. The city remained a pleasant backwater, a small town confined within the limits of its old moated fortifications. The walls have gone now, except for a few pieces of reconstruction, and the city has spread beyond the moat to the river and now edges its way out into the

A samloh, *a bicycle rickshaw in Chiang Mai. They are no longer seen in traffic-choked Bangkok*

surrounding countryside. Yet beside the vastness of Bangkok this is a haven of tranquillity, of tree-lined suburban streets with many of their brick and wood 'colonial' houses still set in their neat gardens.

It is down one such pleasant leafy *soi* that you find Lahmdoun's, an open-air restaurant opposite the Wat Fa Ham temple. This is the place for Kow Soy Noodles, a Thai/Burmese dish that combines crispy fried noodles dunked in a curry and coconut soup. After Bangkok it is strange to be able to eat outside without the ever present traffic fumes and noises. The only noise at Lahmdoun's when I was last there was the somewhat incongruous sound of revivalist hymn-singing from

Top: Si Uah, *spicy sausages grilled over charcoal. Left:* Nam, *Chiang Mai sausage, being wrapped in banana leaves*

an adjacent American mission.

Of course, it is no longer necessary to go to Chiang Mai for Kow Soy Noodles. Inevitably, modern communications and the movement of peoples into the capital has meant a blurring of our regional differences. Once, a visit to the north meant the chance to sample a whole new cuisine, now it is more the opportunity to savour the best of a style of cooking one is already familiar with. However, one element of Thai cooking that still remains uniquely northern is charcuterie. The people of Chiang Mai are the nation's premier pork butchers and sausage-makers and none is better known than Ba Yon or Aunty Yon. I met her when I visited their family house in

The author buying Issan-style grilled chicken with Som Tam, *green papaya salad*

Previous pages: A temple in northern Thailand as dawn breaks

another of the city's quiet back streets and although she is now quite old, she still interests herself in the business she founded. It was her daughter who told me the story of the famous Ba Yon sausage. Ba Yon's husband had been a pork butcher in the days before refrigeration was common in rural Thailand, so that all meat had to be consumed on the day it was slaughtered. Realizing that on bad days they were forced to waste meat, Ba Yon experimented and came up with a recipe that has been much copied since. She mixed ground pork meat with finely chopped pork rind and cooked sticky rice, adding salt, garlic and chilli. This uncooked mix was pressed into a clay pot and sold after three days; no more, no less. This Nam Maw, or sausage in a pot, is 'cooked' from the fermenting effects of the garlic and chilli, much as Tahitian fish is 'cooked' in lemon juice. Although strangers often distrust this method of cooking it is really no worse than eating steak tartare. Later, Ba Yon wrapped her sausage in air-tight packages of banana leaves tied up with bows of slivered bamboo which she sold at the Chiang Mai railway station. Gradually travellers returning to Bangkok began to get in the habit of taking some home as a rare gift from the north. The custom grew of serving Ba Yon's sausage with an aperitif, the round slices being presented with a selection of chopped shallots and raw ginger, salted peanuts, spring onions and coriander leaves and tiny green chillies. As its popularity grew, so did Ba Yon's work. A daughter-in-law tried to open a rival business in Bangkok, to supply the city's supermarkets, but people only wanted the sausage if it bore the name of Ba Yon. To help her family she let the younger woman use her recipe and her name. In Chiang Mai, the original business is still a relatively domestic affair carried out on the ground floor of her home even though much of the grinding and mixing is now done by modern machinery. Hygenic cellophane wrappers have recently been introduced though these are ultimately wrapped in banana leaves for tradition's sake. But even with these new concessions to health, Ba Yon still advises customers to eat the sausage after three days, though her daughter told me that there are certain daredevil gourmets who relish the taste after five days, and are willing to accept the risks involved in satisfying their craving.

Ba Yon's 'raw' sausage is only one of many varieties of Chiang Mai charcuterie. Most are cooked and you can see them grilling and frying on stalls in the Wararot food market near the city's main klong. The smells are delicious. A walk round Wararot reveals the abundance of northern produce and may explain why this of all the Thai regions has not been part of the great drain from the countryside to the capital. Chiang Mai has much to offer its people, but sadly the neighbouring north east has no such bounty. Unlike Chiang Mai with its plentiful rains, the north east has known little but drought in recent years with the result that the Issan peoples of the region have become the country's migrant workers. Many of the fishermen at Hua Hin are today from that once remote area, and how they take to a life on board ship when they come from so far away from the sea I cannot imagine. At the end of our *soi* in Bangkok there is an Issan woman who grills marinated chicken in the character-istic Issan fashion: splayed and gripped in a bamboo fork. No doubt she travelled by crowded bus down the dusty silver Friendship Highway, built by the Americans to service their bases near our border on the Mekong River, during the Vietnam War. To take that route is to pass beyond the ordered world of tourist coaches and international hotels, but there is still much to discover. At Ban Chiang you can see evidence in the form of unique and beautiful pottery of a civilization between 7,000 and 8,000 years old that has only recently been identified. Ban Chiang may be the world's oldest culture. Near the eastern city of Korat is Pimai, in the twelfth century the most westerly outpost of Angkor Wat, the great Khmer temple in Cambodia. Pimai's cave-like galleries have a mysterious air so different from the colourful openness of a Thai temple

Despite the poverty of the region, its people, like all Thais, know how to relax. When I was last in Korat there was a festival in progress and that night everyone gathered at the local sports ground to enjoy the foodstalls, amusement arcades, side-shows and open-air cinema. A favourite attrac-tion was the one-baht dance where in exchange for that small coin the local lads could have a minute's dance with one of the mini-skirted girls provided by the management. Oddly enough, the boys were usually so concerned to show their dancing technique to their watching friends they barely noticed the young ladies swaying along beside them. Sadly, many of these young people will be forced to leave Korat to try to make their way in the big city. It is at this point that the radio and television soap operas have become all too real, the universal struggle of country people to survive in the strange metropolis. One hopeful sign is that the government has recently announced long-term plans to improve agriculture in these once forgotten regions. The leader in these moves has always been our present King, who has made a special point of interesting himself in irrigation schemes. In the grounds of his home in Bangkok, the Chitrilada Palace, he maintains an experimental farm that investigates new dairy processes and tries out new varieties of seeds and plants. His Majesty and his consort Queen Sirikit have taken a special interest in the hill tribes to the north of Chiang Mai, trying to persuade them to adopt crops other than opium. It is a slow, often disappointing process, but one that has to go on if the trade in human misery is to be wiped out. The Queen has done much to promote northern handicrafts as a way of bringing much needed cash into the region. That, and the growth of tourism, should give the peoples of the north some alternative to the production of drugs.

Of course, only the hardiest visitors, willing to go hill trekking, will really see the hill tribes in their remote villages. There are six main groups: Karen, Hmong, Mien, Lahu, Akha and Lisu, and while each has its own language, history and culture, they all share a love of richly-embroidered costumes in vivid colours, often red and black, and love to see their womenfolk weighed down with massive silver ornaments.

The less adventurous can get some idea of mountain life at the various folk spectacles now laid on for visitors to Chiang Mai and while these are inevitably a mere shadow of the

Hill tribes in the North, a group of Akha *women and girls in traditional dress*

*Opium, extracting
the juice from the
poppy*

originals, they are better than nothing. The Old Chiang Mai Cultural Centre puts on a nightly Hill Tribes show following a northern Khan Toke dinner in which visitors sit cross-legged on raised platforms and eat from bowls offering *Nam Prik* with deep fried pork crackling, marinated grilled chicken and a northern curry. This is served with sticky rice so that visitors can try eating with their fingers, rolling the rice into a ball about an inch or so in diameter and using it to lift food from the bowls as desired.

Back in Mr Gee's hamlet at Mae Sae, his son-in-law is eating in exactly that way. The mushrooms he picked that morning have been stir-fried with beans and chillies and are now in a bowl on an enamel tray. Another smaller bowl contains *Nam Prik Num* made with chilli and baby eggplant. Scattered around the tray is a long thin vegetable which has been simply steamed and which can be squeezed open to get at the white beans inside. The tray has been placed on a mat on the floor where husband and wife can sit cross-legged, each with a small woven basket of sticky rice. Their little daughter can take from either as she wishes. The contrast between their stilt house and that of Mr Gee says much about the changes in the region in recent years. Whereas the elder man's home is bare except for a few traditionally hand-crafted objects, this generation has a Phillip's television, a large National radio and, sharing the room with them, a gleaming Honda JX110 – so precious that a second roof has been built inside the thatch to ensure that the rains cannot damage it. Today, the young man not only works his father-in-law's land he also earns money as a gardener at the nearby resorts. One day soon his daughter will go to school where she will learn things beyond her grandfather's wildest imaginings. Between them they span centuries – she is about to enter a world of satellites and nuclear weapons; he remembers when the worst fear was the prowling tiger and the grandest sight was a king on an elephant, like a legend come to life.

STICKY RICE
Khao Niew

Sticky rice is bought by that name and is available in oriental and specialist stores. In Thailand it is often squeezed into a ball with the fingers and then dipped into a sauce.

1 lb/450g/approx 2½cups sticky rice

Put the rice in a bowl or pan, cover with cold water and soak for at least 3 hours (or overnight if possible). Drain and rinse thoroughly. Line the perforated part of a steamer with a double thickness of muslin and turn the rice into it. Put water in the bottom of the steamer and steam the rice over a medium heat for 30 minutes. Turn the rice into a bowl and serve.

'ONG' PORK AND CHILLI SAUCE
Nam Prik Ong

I came across this Nam prik in Chiang Mai. Ong is a northern name that I can't translate. Serve it as a sauce with raw or blanched vegetables, crispy pork crackling (obtainable in many oriental stores), or prawn crackers.

2 tbs/30ml oil
2 garlic cloves, finely chopped
1 tsp/5ml Red curry paste (p. 93)
3oz/90g minced ground pork
1 large tomato, finely chopped
2 tbs/30ml fish sauce
1 tbs/15ml lemon juice
1 tsp/5ml sugar

In a wok or frying pan/skillet, heat the oil until a light haze appears. Add the garlic and fry until golden brown. Mix in the curry paste and cook together briefly. Add the pork, and stir-fry until the meat loses its pink colour. Add the tomato, stir, and cook for 2-3 seconds, then add the fish sauce, lemon juice and sugar. Stir together for 2 minutes to thoroughly blend the flavours.

Turn the mixture into a small bowl and serve.

CHIANG MAI SAUSAGE
Nam

This is similar to the famous Ba Yon sausage. In Thailand we eat this sausage uncooked after it has been cured for 3 days, but I realize that many people will not be keen to eat uncooked pork. For this reason I have followed with this recipe in which the sausage is cooked – it is very delicious and worth the somewhat hard task of preparation.

1 lb/450g pork with skin
6 garlic cloves, finely chopped
1 tsp/5ml salt
2 oz/60g cooked rice
5-6 small whole chillies
Accompaniments:
small lettuce leaves
roasted peanuts
shallots, quartered
garlic cloves, quartered
small fresh chillies, chopped
coriander leaves, coarsely chopped
small lemon wedges

Carefully cut the skin (not the fat) from the meat. Place the skin in a saucepan, cover with water and boil for about 15 minutes. Remove from the pan, drain and dice very small. Remove and discard most of the fat and mince the meat. Thoroughly mix the minced/ground pork with the finely diced skin, garlic, salt, cooked rice and chillies. Press down with the hand, to make sure the mixture is as compressed as possible, then shape into a sausage and roll it tightly in clingfilm. Roll again in foil (we would traditionally use a banana leaf). You should have a very firm sausage. Tie with string or rubber bands and leave in a cool place for 3 days to 'cure'.

After 3 days, unwrap the sausage and cut it into ¼ in/5mm slices. Serve with the listed accompaniments. To eat put a piece of sausage on a lettuce leaf, add any or all of the accompaniments, roll up the leaf and eat.

Opposite: Food from the north east: skewers of grilled marinated pork, moo ping; *sticky rice and a spicy sauce;* som tam *green papaya salad*

SAUSAGE FRIED WITH EGG
Nam Pad Kai

2 tbs/30ml oil

1 garlic clove, finely chopped

1 × 4oz/120g Chiang Mai sausage (p. 138), diced

2 eggs

2 shallots, finely sliced

2 tbs/30ml fish sauce

shaking of ground white pepper

1 large clove pickled garlic (p. 98), sliced

1 medium tomato, cut into wedges

3 spring onions/scallions, coarsely chopped

In a wok or frying pan/skillet, heat the oil and fry the garlic until golden brown. Add the diced sausage, and stir-fry for a few seconds. Break the eggs into the pan, mix briefly, and add the rest of the ingredients, one by one, stirring briskly after each addition. The egg should be thoroughly cooked by this time. Turn onto a serving dish.

SPICY GROUND MEAT
Laab

Browned rice is used to give texture to this dish. It is made from rice which has been 'fried' in a small pan without oil until a pale brown, and then coarsely ground. It keeps well, so make more than you actually need for this recipe, using 3-4 oz/90-120g rice, and remember to keep turning the rice to prevent any of the grains becoming too browned or burnt. It will take 4-5 minutes for the rice to become the right colour.

lettuce, parsley or radish (or any colourful vegetable) for garnish

2 tbs/30ml lemon juice

3 tbs/45ml stock/broth (have more to hand)

2 tbs/30ml fish sauce

½-1 tsp/2.5-5ml chilli powder, depending on taste

4oz/120g minced/ground chicken breast

2 shallots, chopped

½ stalk lemon grass, finely sliced

1 lime leaf, finely sliced

1 tbs/15ml browned rice

1 small spring onion/scallion, chopped

coriander leaves, to garnish

Line a serving dish with the lettuce, parsley or radish. Put the lemon juice, stock, fish sauce and chilli powder in a small pan and heat quickly. Add the chicken and cook quickly until the meat is opaque and cooked through, stirring briskly. Add the shallots, lemon grass, lime leaf, browned rice and spring onion and cook for a few seconds more. Turn the mixture onto the prepared dish and garnish with coriander leaves.

SPICY SAUSAGE
Si Uah

Ask the butcher for pork intestine to use as sausage casings. All the vegetable ingredients for this sausage should be chopped as fine as possible. These quantities should make between 4-6 sausages, depending on their girth and length, and can be doubled or tripled for larger parties. The sausages can also be chilled or frozen for later cooking.

Si Uah, *deep-fried spicy sausage made with pork and spices*

1 lb/450g minced/ground pork (about 15% fat)
2 stalks lemon grass, finely chopped
5 coriander roots, finely chopped
10 lime leaves, finely chopped
2 large garlic cloves, finely chopped
4 shallots, finely chopped
1in/2.5cm piece galangal, finely chopped
2 tbs/30ml Red curry paste (p. 93)
1 tsp/5ml powdered turmeric
½ tsp/2.5ml salt
1 tbs/15ml fish sauce
3 tbs/45ml cooked rice
oil for deep frying

Mix all the ingredients thoroughly together. With the aid of a funnel or a large icing nozzle, force the mixture into the sausage skin, leaving a 2 in/5cm length of unfilled skin in between each 6-8 in/15-20cm of sausage. Try to ensure that the diameter of each sausage is not less than 1 in/2.5cm. Cut in between the sausages to separate them, and knot the unfilled skin at each end of the sausage to make sure the filling won't escape during cooking.

When the sausages are ready, prick them with a fork. Heat oil in deep fryer to medium heat (if the oil is too hot, the sausages are likely to burst). Fry the sausages for 5-6 minutes until well-browned. Remove from oil and drain. Slice diagonally and serve.

SOUR GARLIC SAUSAGE
Si Graw Priow

Ask your butcher for pork intestine to use as sausage casings.

6oz/180g minced/ground pork (about 15% fat)
2oz/60g cooked rice, plain or sticky
2 garlic cloves, finely chopped
¼ tsp/1.25ml salt
½ tsp/2.5ml ground white pepper
Salad:
lettuce
1in/2.5cm piece ginger, finely slivered
3 spring onions/scallions, finely slivered
handful parsley, coarsely chopped
handful coriander leaves, coarsely chopped
1 small red chilli, finely slivered

Thoroughly mix the pork, rice, garlic, salt and pepper. Using a funnel or large icing nozzle, force the mixture into the sausage skin, tying

off each sausage at 1½-2 in/4-5cm lengths. You should have 6-8 small sausages. Cover and leave overnight in a dry warm place (in a cooling oven, or near a radiator; in Thailand they would be left in the sun to dry out partially).

They may be cooked the following day, or stored in the refrigerator for 2-3 days. When you are ready to cook them, prick them with a fork and fry or grill/broil. Combine the salad ingredients and serve with the sausages.

SKEWERED MARINATED PORK
Moo Ping

This makes about 12 skewers, and will serve 4-6 people.

Skewers:
2 garlic cloves, finely chopped
6 coriander roots, finely chopped
4 tbs/60ml fish sauce
1 tbs/15ml light soy sauce
4fl oz/125ml/½ cup thick coconut cream
4fl oz/125ml/½cup oil
1 tbs/15ml sugar
½ tsp/2.5ml ground white pepper
1 lb/450g lean pork, thinly sliced into
1½ × 3in/4 × 7.5cm pieces
Sauce:
1 tbs/15ml fish sauce
2 tbs/30ml lemon juice
1 tbs/15ml light soy sauce
1 tsp/5ml chilli powder
1 tbs/15ml sugar
1 tbs/15ml coarsely chopped coriander

Combine all the skewer ingredients, except the pork, until thoroughly blended. Add the pork and mix in, making sure that each piece is thoroughly coated. Let stand for at least 30 minutes; longer if possible. While the meat is marinating, place all the sauce ingredients in a small bowl and mix well. Taste; if too hot, add more fish sauce, lemon juice and sugar.

Pre-heat the grill/broiler. Take 12 × 6-8in/15-20cm wooden skewers and thread 2 pieces of meat on each, making sure that as much of the surface of the meat as possible will be exposed to the grill. (Make more skewers if you have meat left over.) Grill/broil over a high heat for 2-3 minutes each side, or until the meat is thoroughly cooked through. Serve on a dish garnished with lettuce, parsley or coriander, with the sauce on the side.

CHILLI SOUP
Gaeng Prik

This is a marvellously spicy soup, made even more so with the addition of the optional chilli powder.

10 small dried chillies
2 garlic cloves, chopped
1in/2.5cm piece galangal, chopped
2 shallots, chopped
½ stalk lemon grass, chopped
1 tsp/5ml shrimp paste
¼ tsp/1.5ml ground white pepper
2 pt/1 litre/5 cups stock/broth
4oz/120g lean pork, cut into fine strips
4 tbs/60ml fish sauce
½ tsp/2.5ml sugar
½ tsp/2.5ml chilli powder (optional)
1 tbs/15ml chopped spring onion/scallion
1 tbs/15ml chopped coriander leaf
Serves 6

Using a pestle and mortar or blender, pound or blend the chillies, garlic, galangal, shallots, lemon grass, shrimp paste and pepper together to make a paste. In a large saucepan, bring the stock to the boil. Add 1 tbs/15ml of the pounded mixture and stir to mix well. Add the pieces of pork and bring back to the boil. Skim if necessary. Add the fish sauce, sugar, and chilli powder if you wish. Stir quickly to mix thoroughly. Reduce the heat and simmer for a minute. The meat should be completely cooked through. Pour the soup into a tureen, garnish with the spring onion and coriander and serve.

CHIANG MAI CURRY NOODLE
Kow Soi

4oz/120g fresh *Ba Mee* noodles (p. 86), or use 2oz/60g dry noodles soaked in water for 15 minutes, and drained
2 tbs/30ml oil
1 small garlic clove, finely chopped
1 tsp/5ml Red curry paste (p. 93)
4fl oz/125ml/½cup thick coconut milk
4oz/120g minced/ground pork
½pt/250ml stock/broth
1 tsp/5ml curry powder
¼ tsp/1.5ml turmeric powder
2 tbs/30ml fish sauce
½ tsp/2.5ml sugar
½ tsp/2.5ml lemon juice

To garnish:

1 spring onion/scallion, coarsely chopped
2 shallots, finely diced
1 tbs/15ml pickled cabbage (Gat Pak Dong)
1 lemon, cut into wedges

Bring a pan of water to the boil, and, using a sieve or mesh strainer, dip the noodles into the water for a few seconds. Drain and set aside in a serving bowl. In a wok or frying pan/skillet, heat the oil, add the garlic and fry quickly until golden. Add the curry paste, mix in, and cook for a few seconds. Add the coconut milk, mix in and cook until the liquid starts to reduce. Add the pork and stir thoroughly, then add the stock, curry powder, turmeric, fish sauce, sugar and lemon juice, stirring after each addition. By this time the pork should be cooked through. Cook over a high heat, stirring constantly, for about 10 seconds. Pour the mixture over the noodles, garnish and serve.

SLICED STEAK WITH HOT AND SOUR SAUCE
Nua Yang

lettuce, carrot and cucumber, to garnish
6oz/180g lean steak
1 tbs/15ml lemon juice
1 tbs/15ml fish sauce
1 tsp/5ml sugar
1 tsp/5ml chilli powder
2 shallots, finely sliced
1 small spring onion/scallion, chopped
1 sprig coriander leaf, coarsely chopped

Arrange the lettuce, carrot and cucumber on a serving plate.

Pre-heat the grill/broiler. When really hot, grill/broil the steak so that the meat remains rare on the inside. Slice thinly and set aside. In a bowl, mix together the lemon juice, fish sauce, sugar and chilli powder. Add the shallots, spring onions and the reserved beef. Stir quickly, turn onto the serving dish and sprinkle the coriander leaf over.

Wild mushrooms from the north

SLICED STEAK WITH FRIED GRAINS OF RICE IN A HOT AND SOUR SALAD
Nua Nam Tok

lettuce, cucumber, radish and coriander leaves, to garnish
8oz/230g lean steak
4 tbs/60ml stock/broth
2 tbs/30ml fish sauce
4 tbs/60ml lemon juice
1 tsp/5ml chilli powder
1 tsp/5ml sugar
2 shallots, finely sliced or ½ small onion
1 tbs/15ml browned rice, ground (see p. 140)

Prepare a serving plate with lettuce, cucumber, radish and coriander leaves.

Pre-heat the grill/broiler. When really hot, grill/broil the steak quickly – the meat should be quite rare in the middle. Slice it thinly and set aside. Put the stock, fish sauce, lemon juice, chilli powder and sugar in a small pan over a high heat. Stir quickly and bring to the boil. Add the steak and stir; add the shallot and stir, then add the ground rice and stir once to mix. Cook for a second, then turn the mixture onto the prepared plate and serve.

GREEN PAPAYA SALAD
Som Tam

Green papaya is a firm fruit. Traditionally we would pound it gently in a clay mortar to soften the fibres and blend it with the other ingredients. But this can also be achieved by mixing and squeezing it gently with a spoon in a bowl. If green papaya is not available, grated carrot could be substituted, as could very finely shredded white cabbage; a mixture of papaya and carrot looks attractive and tastes good. Use a hand grater for this recipe, sliding the vegetable down its whole length in order to obtain the longest possible gratings.

lettuce and parsley, to garnish
4oz/120g grated raw green papaya
1 small garlic clove
1 tbs/15ml roasted peanuts (if you have no mortar these should be roughly ground)
1 tbs/15ml dried shrimp, ground
2 medium green or red chillies, chopped
4-5 green beans, coarsely chopped
1 medium tomato, sliced
1 tbs/15ml sugar
2 tbs/30ml fish sauce
2 tbs/30ml lemon juice

Line a serving plate with lettuce and parsley. Pound the papaya with the garlic. With a pestle and mortar, or in a bowl, gently mix all the ingredients together, beginning with the hardest and then adding the liquids. Alternate pounding and turning with a spoon until all are thoroughly blended. Turn onto serving dish.

CHIANG MAI CURRY
Gaeng Hang Lay

2 tbs/30ml oil
1 small garlic clove, chopped
1 tbs/15ml Red curry paste (p. 93)
4fl oz/125ml/½cup thick coconut milk, or evaporated milk
4oz/120g lean pork, finely slivered
1in/2.5cm piece ginger, finely chopped
2 tbs/30ml stock/broth or water
2 tbs/30ml fish sauce
1 tsp/5ml sugar
½ tsp/2.5ml turmeric powder
2 tsp/10ml lemon juice
4 cloves pickled garlic, coarsely chopped (p. 98)

In a wok or frying pan, heat the oil until a light haze appears. Add the garlic and fry until golden brown. Add the curry paste, mix in and cook for a few seconds. Stir in the coconut milk, and cook until the liquid starts to reduce. Add the pork, stir well to coat the meat and cook for a few seconds. Add the ginger, stir and mix. Stirring quickly after each addition, add the stock or water, fish sauce, sugar, turmeric and lemon juice. Stir and cook for a minute or two until you are sure the meat has cooked through. Add the pickled garlic, stir to mix, and turn into a serving bowl.

CHICKEN WITH LEMON GRASS CURRY
Ook Gai

Obviously, it is preferable to make a fresh curry paste as below, but if you are in a hurry and crave the flavour of lemon grass, then substitute a tablespoonful of Red curry paste (p. 93) and add a teaspoon of turmeric powder.

Curry paste:

1 stalk lemon grass, coarsely chopped
1in/2.5 piece galangal, coarsely chopped
2 lime leaves, chopped
3 shallots, coarsely chopped
6 coriander roots, coarsely chopped
2 garlic cloves
4 dried long red chillies, deseeded and coarsely chopped
1 tsp/5ml shrimp paste
1 tsp/5ml turmeric powder

Chicken curry:

3 tbs/45ml oil
2 garlic cloves, finely chopped
12oz/350g chicken on the bone, (eg. thigh), chopped into small pieces
3 tbs/45ml fish sauce
about 4fl oz/125ml/½cup stock/broth or water
1 tsp/5ml sugar
1 stalk lemon grass, chopped into 3-4 pieces and gently crushed
5 lime leaves, finely sliced

With a pestle and mortar or blender, pound or blend all the ingredients for the curry paste together until smooth. Prepare the chicken curry. In a wok or frying pan, heat the oil until a light haze appears. Add the chopped garlic and fry until golden brown. Add 1 tbs/15ml of the curry paste (or Red curry paste plus 1 tsp/5ml turmeric powder), stir together and cook briefly – 4-5 seconds. Add the chicken pieces and stir, ensuring that each piece of chicken is thoroughly coated with the curry mixture. Add the fish sauce, stock or water and sugar and stir to mix. Add the lemon grass and lime leaves, stir, lower the heat and simmer gently for 15-20 minutes. If the mixture should become too dry, add a little more stock, though the final result should be quite dry. Turn onto a serving dish.

Previous pages: Chiang Mai Khan Toke dinner: Nam Prik Ong with crispy pork and raw vegetables; Ook Gai, chicken with lemon grass curry; Laab and sticky rice

HOT SPICED EEL
Pad Pet Pla Lai

The original recipe calls for 30 fresh chillies and 10 dried, but this is too much even for some Thai palates – including my own – and I have reduced the amount of chilli considerably. Even so, it is a hot dish. You can substitute whitebait (not too small) for the eel. Again, if you are pressed for time, 1 tablespoon of Red curry paste (p. 93) can be substituted for the paste below.

Paste:

4 small red or green chillies, chopped
2 dried long red chillies, deseeded and chopped
2 shallots, coarsely chopped
2 garlic cloves
1in/2.5cm piece galangal, coarsely chopped
½ stalk lemon grass, coarsely chopped
1 tsp/5ml chopped kaffir lime skin (p. 38), or 1 lime leaf, chopped
½ tsp/2.5ml salt
1 tsp/5ml shrimp paste

3 tbs/45ml oil
12oz/340g eel, cut into chunks, or whole whitebait
2 fresh peppercorns, or 2 tsp/10ml bottled green peppercorns
4 tbs/60 ml stock/broth or water
2 tbs/30ml fish sauce
½ tsp/2.5ml sugar
2 small green aubergines/eggplant, quartered (optional)
10 holy basil leaves
1 tbs/15ml slivered krachai, if available (if using dry, soak in water to soften before use)
1 lime leaf, finely slivered

Using a pestle and mortar or blender, pound or blend all the paste ingredients together until smooth. In a wok or frying pan, heat the oil until a light haze appears. Add 1 tbs/15ml of the above paste (or Red curry paste) and fry together briefly. Add the eel pieces, turning them to ensure they are covered with the paste, and cook briefly, making sure they don't stick to the pan. Add the peppercorns, stock or water, fish sauce, sugar and aubergines (if liked), one by one, stirring after each addition. The eel should be nearly cooked through. Cook for a few more seconds. Add the basil leaves and krachai, stir and mix. Finally, add the lime leaf. Stir once more.

FROG WITH SWEET BASIL LEAF
Gob Pad Krapow

This is a hot dish made with frog meat. If this is not to your taste, then chicken may be substituted. The small chillies are, of course, very hot and with the basil leaves the dish becomes very sharp indeed.

3 tbs/45ml oil
3 garlic cloves, finely chopped
6oz/180g minced/ground frog or chicken meat
3 small red chillies, finely chopped
2 tbs/30ml fish sauce
1 tbs/15ml light soy sauce
1 tsp/5ml sugar
4 tbs/60ml stock/broth or water
15-20 sweet basil leaves

In a wok or frying pan, heat the oil until a light haze appears. Fry the chopped garlic until golden brown. Add the frog or chicken meat and the chopped chillies and cook for 1 minute or less, stirring briskly. Add the fish sauce, soy sauce, sugar and stock or water, and continue to cook, stirring, for 1-2 minutes until the meat is cooked through. Add the basil leaves, stir and cook for a few seconds, then turn onto a serving dish.

STEAMED FISH WITH CHILLI SAUCE
Pla Nung Jeow Prik

Since this region has no coastline, freshwater fish is normally used. The sauce is quite pungent and the slightly charred flavour distinctive.

Sauce:
5 dried long red chillies
5 shallots, peeled
4 garlic cloves, peeled
2 medium tomatoes
2 tbs/30ml fish sauce
1 tsp/5ml lemon juice
1 whole fish (eg. trout)
2-3 leaves lettuce, cabbage or spinach

Heat the grill/broiler, and when very hot, grill/broil the chillies, shallots, garlic and tomatoes together on a piece of foil, turning occasionally with tongs, until the skins start to blister and become charred (about 6-8 minutes). Using a pestle and mortar or food processor, pound or blend them all together,

Dicing vegetables, hill-tribe style

and add the fish sauce and lemon juice. Mix together and set aside. On a dish that will fit inside your steamer, lie the fish on top of a bed of the vegetable leaves. Steam for 10-15 minutes until the fish is cooked through. Serve the fish on the dish on which it was cooked with the sauce in a small bowl on the side.

STEAMED FISH IN BANANA LEAF
Oo Pla

In Thailand we would certainly use a banana leaf, which imparts a delicate and subtle flavour, to hold the fish, but a bowl or other suitable dish is an acceptable alternative.

5 dried long red chillies, deseeded and soaked in water to soften
2 garlic cloves, chopped
2 shallots, coarsely chopped
1in/2.5cm piece galangal, coarsely chopped
1 tbs/15ml chopped lemon grass
1 tbs/15ml shrimp paste
12oz-1 lb/350-450g freshwater or other fish, filleted and cut into small pieces
2 tbs/30ml fish sauce
20 basil leaves

Using pestle and mortar or blender, pound or blend together the chillies, garlic, shallots, galangal, lemon grass and shrimp paste. Add the fish pieces, the fish sauce and the basil leaves to this mixture and mix together gently. Put the mixture in a bowl (or wrap in banana leaf, securing the 'package' with toothpicks) and steam for 15 minutes from the time the steamer water has started to boil.

RITES OF PASSAGE

FOOD FOR SPECIAL OCCASIONS.
THAI DESSERTS.
FRUIT AND VEGETABLE CARVING.

ost people travelling home to Bangkok from Hua Hin seize the opportunity to break their journey in Phetchaburi. Few bother to go into the town, the real attraction lies just off the main highway in a large concrete building that is half-restaurant, half-supermarket – whose speciality is the wide range of Thai sweets and preserves that most people can't be bothered to make for themselves. The visitors usually enjoy an ice-cream or some sugared fruits, or perhaps a baked custard before stocking up with packets and boxes to be enjoyed later at home or offered to friends as gifts. My family's especial favourite is a variety of *Kanom Maw Gaeng* – literally 'sweet curry in a pot', a name which doesn't bear the slightest resemblance to what is in effect a two-layered baked custard of moong beans, egg, sugar and coconut, flavoured and decorated with lotus seeds. Actually, *Kanom Maw Gaeng* is one of the easier Thai sweets to make but the owners of the shop have realized that, as in the West, confectionery is an art few people wish to practise and so their business thrives. Just as in

The little King of Thailand, Ananda Mahidol, Rama VIII, dressed for court ceremonial in the 1930s

Europe, Thai sweets make up an entire form of cooking in their own right. They can be divided into liquid and dry, the liquid being the many varieties of fruit and vegetables, sometimes raw but more often boiled and served in sweetened coconut milk or a rich syrup; while the dry are really small cakes or *Kanom* made from sweetened pastes and jellies. Some of these are incredibly complex and best left to the professionals but others are easier to make while still looking impressive and are a fascinating way to end a Thai meal.

The same underlying principles apply to Thai confectionery as to our savoury dishes, namely the need to balance elements such as sweet and sour or soft and crunchy. The classic example is 'Mango with sticky rice' where the intense sweetness of the ripe fruit is offset by a slightly salty coconut cream poured over the rice. It often amazes foreigners to see young Thais tipping salt into a glass of coca-cola but this is just that principle being put into effect in new circumstances.

Loaded down with boxes of baked and steamed sweets and with packets of crystallized fruits, the travellers head back to the capital but it is a pity few take the opportunity to get to know the town, for Phetchaburi has much to offer the visitor. On a hill facing the sweet supermarket is a gleaming white palace, recently restored and opened to the public. It is a *fin de siècle* gem, half European, half Oriental, built by King Mongkut, our great reforming monarch who began the process of turning

Previous pages: A parade during the Yasothon rocket festival ends at a temple

Siam into a modern nation. Sadly, this noble man had the misfortune to hire an English governess, Anna Leonowens, to teach the royal princes. It is not known if he ever met her, for she had hardly arrived at the palace before home sickness drove her back to England. Short of money, she wrote a fanciful account of the 'exotic' court of which she claimed to have been a privileged member and this has come down to us as *The King and I*. The real King Mongkut was a saintly man who spent much of his life as a monk, but Yul Brynner's portrayal is probably the only image most people have of my country. Not that we are unduly upset by the film; though it is banned in Thailand out of respect for the King's memory, almost every Thai who travels abroad has seen it and enjoyed it as a piece of fiction which has as much to do with our country as a film about the planet Mars.

The real Siam can be found not far from King Mongkut's palace on the outskirts of Phetchaburi, after a fairly long walk up a steep tree-lined slope to the Khao Luang Cave. In the cavernous interior are huge stalactites eerily lit by a shaft of

The statue of the Emerald Buddha, the most sacred shrine in Thailand

Intricately carved fruits: crab apple, papaya, rose apple and water melon transformed into flowers

natural light. We Thais look on caves as ready-made temples and fill them with Buddha images and this particular cavern has many, glistening in the half-light. Phetchaburi also has a marvellous man-made temple complex, part of which predates the founding of Bangkok and so gives some idea of the glories of Thai art and architecture before the Burmese destroyed Ayuthaya in the eighteenth century. The façades of Wat Mahathat are covered with intricately carved stucco work like some fabulous oriental wedding cake, but the interior of the ordination hall glows with murals of Thai life, wonderfully detailed paintings that are presently threatened by the destructive effects of damp and are in urgent need of restoration.

Most of the great occasions in Thai life, whether personal or national, have a religious element. Before the establishment of the European Sunday, we had a continuous working week broken up by many Temple holy days usually ordained by the lunar calendar. Today we have a five- or six-day working week with a number of national holidays, half religious, half royal or patriotic, though even they usually involve some sort of Buddhist rite. April the sixth, for example, is Chakri Day when we celebrate the founding of the present dynasty and people in Bangkok try to take flowers and incense to the Temple of the Emerald Buddha and then visit the nearby Pantheon of Royal Statues which is opened only on that one day. The King is the focus of many holidays. His Majesty's birthday, the anniversary of his coronation and the Queen's birthday are all National Holidays celebrated with parades and fireworks. It is during these great national events when the King hosts a reception or a banquet that Thai food is seen in its most exalted form with incredible attention played to the beauty of presentation. This means not only that the food should be stylishly set out on fine dishes but that it is also decorated with exquisitely carved fruit and vegetables. All Thai cooks decorate their food, though on an everyday basis this usually means little more than garnishing a plate with a simple flower made out of a finely sliced chilli or a sculpted carrot. These, however, are mere echoes of the splendid arrangements that the true fruit and vegetable carver can aspire to. The dullest vegetables are finely sliced, peeled back, carved and bent in a sort of origami to become delicate bouquets of flowers, so that the diner is initially fooled into thinking that the plate is festooned with blossom. For great occasions, the court has the services of a Royal Carver, an hereditary post held today by Khun Chan. His family have lived and worked in one of the old wooden houses in the narrow streets within the Grand Palace complex since it was built after the founding of the city two hundred years ago. Khun Chan, as his fathers before him, carves the fruit and vegetables for the royal table though today he is no longer a direct servant of the court. Because the King now lives in the more modest circumstances of the Chitrilada Palace leading the life of a busy Head of State, Khun Chan's services are only required for special occasions. However, because of his family's connection with an earlier age he is allowed to go on living in the old palace from where he provides decorations for banquets given by major businesses or for reception at the city's luxury hotels.

Even when it is not beautifully sculpted, fruit in Thailand is always served peeled, sliced and pleasingly arranged on a plate or in a dish. For most people fruit is the principal dessert. It is plentiful and very, very cheap and is also a soothing end to a hot meal. Thailand is fortunate in having an incredible array of tropical fruit of the highest quality, a fact that is now becoming known elsewhere as our exports rapidly expand. Most major cities in the West now have Thai fruit on sale somewhere and knowledge of tropical fruit has spread beyond the inevitable pineapple and lychee to include papaya, and the indescribably delicious mangosteen. Sadly, the majority of mangoes in the West still come from other sources so the unparalleled

Opening a durian to extract the sweet custardy segments, delicious despite the smell!

deliciousness of the far sweeter Thai variety is little known. But although foreigners may now be eating rambutan and pomelo there still remains one fruit that is a mystery to all but its avid band of devotees, the durian. Looking like an outsize green hand-grenade or a sort of rugby ball with spikes, the durian is that peculiar fruit that exudes a bad odour when split open to get at its custardy innards. Polite people describe the smell as something like rotten cheese, but that is putting it mildly – it is like a hot day at a sewage farm. Only when you have managed to fight back your feelings of nausea and tasted the creamy flesh inside you can begin to appreciate why people cannot live without it. Nevertheless you will also understand why Thai Inter forbids passengers to carry the fruit on its flights. Happily, most tropical fruits are small, delicately flavoured and scented.

Fruits always form part of any offering that we make whether to the spirit house or to Buddha. If there is a special occasion such as the blessing of an altar in a new house then the visiting monks will be offered whatever is best in season. On all occasions that involve a party, fruit and sweetmeats will be set out in pretty patterns on raised dishes. This is especially the case at the two biggest events in any Thai life: when a son

Dressed like a bride, a country boy becomes a monk during the rainy season

Previous pages: Fireworks over Bangkok to celebrate the King's sixtieth birthday

Look Choob:
*deceptive sweets
moulded to look like
tiny vegetables*

becomes a monk for a short period and when someone in the family marries. Nearly all Thai males enter a monastery at some time, even the present King did so as a young man. When I became a monk in 1973 my family invited relatives and friends to celebrate on the day before I entered the monastery and on the day itself food was taken to the temple as a gift for the monks. On arrival my parents symbolically clipped my hair before one of the monks shaved my head and a period of abstinence began in which I begged for my food and ate the final meal of the day at the end of the morning. In Bangkok the food offered to visitors on this occasion is relatively modest compared to the lavish feasting in the countryside. I once visited the village of Si Satchenali in the centre of Thailand to see the celebrations when the boys entered the monastery and was overwhelmed at the scale of the ceremony. On the previous day, every woman in the village was cooking; great vats of rice were being boiled up under the stilt houses; and every home was willingly offering its best to any visitor who cared to call. The next day, the boys were shaved and sumptuously dressed, and each had his own elephant to carry him in a great procession round the village accompanied by anyone who could move, or rather, dance. It was a spectacle out of the past that slowly wound its way to the temple.

The one occasion when the capital rivals the countryside is a wedding. Still in Thailand, the union of a man and a woman really means the union of two families and the setting up of a complex set of relationships very important in a culture where families are still expected to help each other a great deal. Thus a wedding is a major public statement. My youngest brother Ooie's wedding was the most recent in my immediate family and although it was not on the scale of the great social weddings made among the big business families that we read about in newspapers, it lacked nothing in terms of cramming as many occasions to eat and drink as possible into twenty-four hours. We began in the morning when my family accompanied

Ooie from our house to his fiancée's home, each of us bearing gifts of sweetmeats, flowers and presents. Both families were now formally introduced to each other and the young couple paid their respects to the oldest members of both groups. Throughout, there was a constant flow of delicacies for everyone. After about an hour an official came from the town hall to complete the civil formalities and then a group of monks from a nearby temple came to bless the union and accept food. At the end of the morning we took our brother back home, for although he was legally married, the true marriage occurs only when the bride is formally brought back to our house, and that would be later. That afternoon, the arrangements were a mix of a traditional Thai and a modern Western marriage. Relatives and friends were invited to one of the main luxury hotels where two large reception rooms had been booked. Ooie wore his dress uniform as a newly qualified police officer and Aw, his wife, wore the full length white dress of a European wedding. After standing on line to receive members of the immediate family, they moved to a raised dais at the end of the first room where they knelt at prayer stools so that all could pass and sprinkle lustral water on their hands and wish them well. After that, everyone moved to the adjoining room to which friends and colleagues had been invited, and a full-blown reception with food, drink, toasts, speeches, and cake-cutting took place. As I have said elsewhere, traditionally we did not have hors d'oeuvres or snacks or cocktail food as such, rather the earliest cooked dishes were brought out to be 'tasted' with drinks. Now, however, we have adopted the habit of having something small to nibble before the meal proper begins or as 'finger-food' for parties, and a whole range of Thai appetizers has been developed.

Weddings are also occasions to serve the most refined of Thai sweets, Look Choob, which were once served only to the Kings of Siam and their court. They are so delicate and difficult to make that nowadays there are few left who are skilled at the task. The word 'look' can mean fruit and 'choob' means to dip, and to make Look Choob you mix a paste of soya beans, sugar and coconut juice that tastes like marzipan and fashion it into deceptive miniature replicas of fruit and vegetables, tiny bright red chillies, little baby eggplant, cherries and grapes, which are then coloured and dipped in clear gelatin to provide a waxy glaze, so that at a glance it is impossible to realize that they are not real. The fun lies in popping a whole 'chilli' into your mouth yet eating something deliciously sweet. Look Choob are still served on Royal occasions but ordinary folk like to have them for their wedding receptions even though they are very expensive.

After my brother's reception our family took the newly-weds to our home with members of the bride's family as guests, and supper was served – a thick soup of polished rice to complete the day's eating. Then the longest married couple in our family went to the newly decorated bedroom and lay on the marriage

bed for a few moments to bring the blessings of a long marriage. After that, Ooie and Aw were brought to the room blessed by their parents and everyone retired.

A wedding like that is probably the biggest feast a modern family lays on today, but if they are not so lavish almost every important event in our lives is an excuse for food. And not only our lives! For even when we are dead there is a meal to celebrate our going. Our funeral arrangements are very prolonged and the coffin is kept in a temple chapel so that many nights of prayer can take place before the cremation. Because people come straight from work it is not thought peculiar that food should be offered. Non-Thais find the sight of a Thai family contentedly supping soup in the presence of their deceased loved one slightly gruesome. They shouldn't worry. Being Thai, the dead relation would fully understand that you must eat to live and that whatever the occasion you might as well enjoy it.

Traditional wedding, the bride and groom accept good wishes and gifts from their neighbours

HORS D'OEUVRES OR PARTY SNACKS

STUFFED TOMATOES
Sida

The filling here is the northern Laab from Chapter 7. For a really impressive version, you can use the tiny cherry tomatoes: there won't be much laab in each, but scattered among the other hors d'oeuvres they will look very attractive.

12 small tomatoes
2 tbs/30ml lemon juice
3 tbs/45ml stock/broth
2 tbs/30ml fish sauce
½-1 tsp/2.5-5ml chilli powder, depending on taste
4oz/120g minced/ground chicken breast
2 shallots, finely chopped
½ stalk lemon grass, finely chopped
1 lime leaf, finely chopped
1 tbs/15ml rice, browned and ground (p. 140)
1 small spring onion/scallion, finely chopped
coriander leaves, to garnish

Turn the tomatoes upside down so that the stalk is at the bottom. Slice what is now the tops off the tomatoes with a sharp knife to serrate edges. Scoop out the pulp and seeds.

In a small pan, quickly heat the lemon juice, stock, fish sauce and chilli powder. Add the chicken and cook quickly until the meat is opaque and cooked through, stirring briskly. Add the shallots, lemon grass, lime leaf, browned rice and spring onion and cook for a few seconds. The mixture should not be too liquid. Remove from the heat. Spoon into the tomato shells, garnish with coriander leaves and serve.

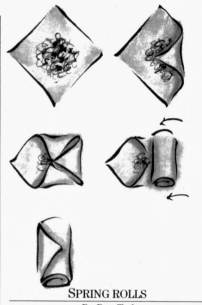

SPRING ROLLS
Po Pea Tod

Thai spring rolls are delicate and compact compared to the looser Chinese and Vietnamese versions. They are also rather mildly flavoured, and the sweet sauce is an essential accompaniment.

2 tbs/30ml flour
6 spring roll sheets (approx 10 in/25cm square)
2oz/60g dry *Wun Sen* noodles (p. 86), soaked in cold water until soft (about 4oz/120g wet weight)
about 8 pieces dried mushroom, soaked in cold water to soften and chopped very fine
4oz/120g minced/ground pork (omit for a vegetarian roll)
2 garlic cloves, finely chopped
2 tbs/30ml fish sauce
2 tbs/30ml light soy sauce
½ tsp/2.5ml sugar
ground white pepper
oil for deep frying

Opposite: Pork toasts, stuffed cucumber, gold bags, stuffed tomatoes, spring rolls, pork balls wrapped in noodles

Sauce:
4 tbs/60ml sugar
6 tbs/90ml rice vinegar
½ tsp/2.5ml salt
1 small red chilli, finely chopped
1 small green chilli, finely chopped

Combine the flour with 4 tbs/60ml water. Heat the flour and water together, stirring, until thick and clear. Pour into a saucer and set aside.

If making small spring rolls, cut each sheet into 4 equal pieces.

Drain the vermicelli and, using scissors, chop into very small pieces. Place in a bowl and mix thoroughly with the finely chopped mushroom, minced pork (if using), garlic, fish sauce, soy sauce, sugar and a shaking of pepper. On each sheet place 1½-2 tbs/25-30ml of the mixture (1 heaped teaspoon if making small rolls) fold in 3 corners to make an envelope and wrap tightly. Seal the joins tightly with the flour and water paste. At this point the rolls can be chilled or frozen for future use. Otherwise, heat oil in a deep-fryer until a light haze appears. Deep-fry the rolls until golden brown.

Make the sauce. Boil the sugar, rice vinegar and salt together in a small pan until the sugar has dissolved and the mixture thickens. Divide the syrup into two portions and add the chopped chillies to one of them. Serve the rolls on a plate with the sauces on the side for dipping.

PORK SARONG (PORK BALLS WRAPPED IN NOODLES)
Moo Sarong

Serve these with the same sauce used for Spring Rolls (left), made in the same way, in two portions.

3 garlic cloves
3 coriander roots
1 nest Ba Mee noodles (p. 86), fresh or dry
6oz/180g minced/ground pork
1 egg
ground white pepper
½ tsp/2.5ml salt
1 tbs/15ml light soy sauce
1 tsp/5ml sugar
oil for deep frying

Pound or blend the garlic with the coriander roots. Boil a pan of water and, using a strainer or long-handled sieve, douse the noodles in the boiling water for about 5 seconds – longer if using dry noodles – to soften and separate the threads. Rinse immediately in cold water, drain and set aside.

In a bowl mix the pork with the pounded garlic and coriander, the egg, a shaking of pepper, salt, soy sauce and the sugar. Form the mixture into small balls, about ¾ in/2cm in diameter. Lift 3-4 strands of noodle and use to wrap each ball, winding the strands into a mesh which thickly covers the pork. This is a rather time-consuming process and requires some patience. You should have about 12 wrapped balls. Heat the oil until a light haze appears and deep-fry the wrapped balls until golden brown. Drain and serve with the sauce.

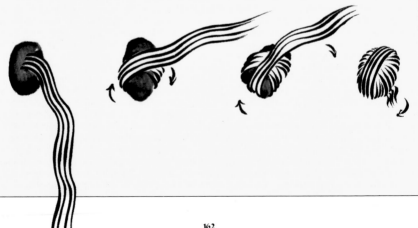

SWEETCORN CAKE
Tod Man Khao Pohd

12 oz/340g sweetcorn (canned or frozen: if
using canned, drain well)
1 tbs/15ml curry powder
2 tbs/30ml rice flour
3 tbs/45ml wheat flour
½ tsp/2.5ml salt
2 tbs/30ml light soy sauce
oil for deep frying
Sauce:
4 tbs/60ml rice vinegar
2 tbs/30ml sugar
1in/2.5cm piece cucumber, quartered
lengthwise, then finely sliced
½ small carrot, halved lengthwise, then
finely sliced
2 shallots, finely sliced
1 tbs/15ml ground roasted peanuts
1 small red or green chilli, finely sliced

Mix all the ingredients (except the oil)
together. Heat the oil in a deep-fryer. Using a
tablespoon, take a spoonful of the mixture at a
time, compressing each one slightly with the
fingers to make a small cake, and slide into the
hot oil. Fry until deep golden brown. Remove
the cakes with a slotted spoon and drain.

Make the sauce. Boil the vinegar and sugar
together in a small pan, stirring constantly,
until the sugar dissolves and the mixture
begins to thicken slightly. Remove from heat
and allow to cool. Pour into a small bowl, add
the remaining ingredients and stir to mix.
Serve with the cakes.

CHICKEN SATAY
Satay

Satay is now as universal as the hamburger.
Malaysian satay was originally introduced into
our cuisine via our southern, Muslim region.
These satays can also be made with pork or
beef.

1 tsp/5ml coriander seeds
1 tsp/5ml cumin seeds
3 chicken breasts
2 tbs/30ml light soy sauce
1 tsp/5ml salt
4 tbs/60ml oil
1 tbs/15ml curry powder
1 tbs/15ml ground turmeric
8 tbs/120ml coconut milk
3 tbs/45ml sugar

Roast the coriander and cumin seeds gently
in a small frying pan without oil for about
5 minutes, stirring and shaking to ensure
they don't burn. Remove from the heat and
grind together to make a fine powder. (You
could substitute ready-ground seeds if more
convenient.)

With a sharp knife, cut the chicken breasts
into fine slices (3in/7.5cm long × 1½in/4cm
wide × ¼in/5mm thick). Put the slices in a
bowl and add all the remaining ingredients,
including the ground coriander and cumin.
Mix thoroughly and stand overnight, or for 8
hours (you can prepare in the morning for the
evening's meal).

Pre-heat the grill/broiler (we would normally use a charcoal or barbecue grill). Using
7-8in/18-20cm wooden satay sticks, thread 2
pieces of the marinated meat on each stick –
not straight through the meat, but rather as if
you were gathering or smocking a piece of
material. Grill/broil the satays until the meat is
cooked through – about 6-8 minutes – turning
to make sure they are browned on both sides.
Serve with Peanut Sauce and Cucumber
Pickle.

PEANUT SAUCE

2 tbs/30ml oil
3 garlic cloves, finely chopped
1 tbs/15ml Massaman (p. 93) or Red curry
paste (p. 93)
8 tbs/120ml coconut milk
8fl oz/250ml/1cup stock/broth
1 tbs/15ml sugar
1 tsp/5ml salt
1 tbs/15ml lemon juice
4 tbs/60ml crushed roasted peanuts (or
peanut butter)
4 tbs/60ml dried breadcrumbs

In a frying pan/skillet, heat the oil until a light
haze appears. Add the chopped garlic and fry
until golden brown. Add the curry paste, mix
well and cook together for a few seconds. Add
the coconut milk, mix in well and cook for a
few seconds. Add the stock, sugar, salt and
lemon juice, and stir to blend. Cook for a
minute or two, constantly stirring. Add the
ground peanuts and breadcrumbs, stir to
blend thoroughly and pour the sauce into a
bowl.

CUCUMBER PICKLE
A Jad

4 tbs/60ml rice vinegar
1 tsp/5ml sugar
2 tbs/30ml finely chopped cucumber
2 shallots, finely sliced
1 small carrot, finely chopped
1 small red or green chilli, finely chopped

Mix all the ingredients in a small bowl and serve.

PRAWN WRAPPED IN BEAN CURD SHEET
Heh Guen

2 garlic cloves
2 coriander roots
6oz/120g peeled prawns, coarsely chopped
1oz/30g pork fat, finely chopped
good shaking of ground white pepper
1 egg
4-5 bean curd sheets (p. 37), soaked in cold water for 8-10 minutes until soft
oil for deep frying
Sweet and Sour Plum Sauce:
4fl oz/120ml rice vinegar
4fl oz/120ml sugar
1 tsp/5ml preserved plum, stoned

Pound the garlic with the coriander roots. Thoroughly mix together the chopped prawns, pork fat, garlic and coriander mixture, white pepper and the egg. Divide the mixture into 4-5 portions. Wrap each portion in a softened bean curd sheet, making a 'spring roll' shape about 5-6in/13-15cm long. The bean curd sheets need to be handled carefully, as they tend to tear, but you can 'patch' as necessary. You should finish with about 3 thicknesses of sheet around the pork mixture; make sure you fold the ends in to enclose the mixture.

Steam the rolls for about 10 minutes: you will find that the bean curd sheet tightens about the mixture. Remove and cool. The rolls can now be set aside for frying later on, or wrapped and stored in the refrigerator for frying the following day. They may also be frozen.

Make the sauce. Boil the vinegar and sugar together to make a thick syrup. Add the plum and break it up in the syrup, stir thoroughly to mix. Cool. To finish, cut each roll into 5-6 rounds or diagonal pieces. Heat the oil in the deep-fryer until a light haze appears, then deep-fry the pieces until golden brown. Remove and drain. Serve with the Sweet and sour plum sauce.

PRAWNS IN BATTER WITH TWO SAUCES (SERVES 2-4)
Gung Chup Bang Tod

12 large prawns, beheaded, shelled and deveined, but with tail shell left on
oil for deep frying
Batter:
5oz/145g/1cup wheat flour
½ tsp/2.5ml salt
1 egg
8fl oz/250ml/1cup water
Sauce 1:
4 tbs/60ml rice vinegar
4 tbs/60ml sugar
¼ tsp/1.25ml salt
1 small red or green chilli, finely chopped
Sauce 2:
3 tbs light soy sauce
5-6 coriander leaves, coarsely chopped

Spring onions, (scallions)

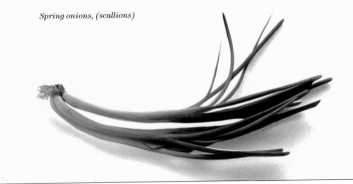

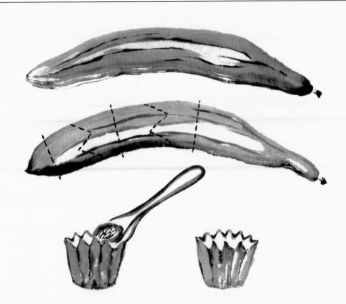

Preparing cucumber cups

Make the batter. In a bowl mix the flour and salt. Break the egg into the mixture, and mix thoroughly. Add the water gradually, whisking the mixture constantly. You should have a thick creamy batter. Heat the oil until a light haze appears. Dip each prawn into the batter, making sure it is thoroughly coated, and drop into the hot oil. Deep-fry until golden brown. Remove with a strainer or slotted spoon and place on serving dish.

Make sauce 1. In a small saucepan, boil the vinegar and sugar together until the sugar dissolves and forms a syrup. Add the salt and stir. Remove from the heat, cool, and add the chopped chilli. Pour into a small bowl. Make sauce 2. Mix the soy sauce with the coriander leaves and pour into a small bowl.

The fried prawns should be dipped by the tail into either sauce. The batter and sauces can also be used for fried strips of vegetable (carrot, celery, beans, courgettes/zuccini etc.)

CUCUMBER STUFFED WITH BEEF
Yam Nua Saweoy

Saweoy is a 'royal' word that means eat. Using courtly language in this context implies something that is small and pretty, and usually delicately carved.

1 cucumber, as long as possible, trimmed at each end and cut into 1in/2.5cm thick slices
6oz/180g lean steak
1 spring onion/scallion, finely chopped
2 tbs/30ml lemon juice
2 tbs/30ml fish sauce
1 small red chilli, finely chopped
1 tsp/5ml sugar
¼ tsp/1.25ml salt
coriander leaves, to garnish

Pre-heat the grill/broiler. Cut the cucumber into sections making alternate straight and zig zag cuts – one cucumber will provide several cups. Using a sharp-edged spoon scoop out the centre of each piece of cucumber.

Grill/broil the steak medium rare. Chop into fine pieces. Mix with the rest of the ingredients. Spoon into the cucumber cups, garnish with coriander leaves.

Wrapping gold bags

PORK TOASTS
Kanom Bang Na Moo

5 slices day-old bread
2 garlic cloves, finely chopped
3 coriander roots, chopped
4oz/120g minced/ground pork
2 eggs
2 tbs/30ml fish sauce
pinch of ground white pepper
1 tbs/15ml milk or cold water
oil for deep frying
coriander leaves, quartered cucumber, finely sliced rings of red chilli etc., to garnish
Serves 4-6

Pre-heat the oven to 120°C/250°F/Gas ½. Trim the crusts off the bread and cut each slice into 4 (or cut into decorative shapes using a pastry cutter). Lay the pieces on a baking sheet/cookie tray and put in the oven for about 10 minutes until they start to crisp. Remove from the oven.

In the meantime, with a pestle and mortar or blender, pound or blend the garlic and coriander roots together. In a bowl combine this mixture with the pork, 1 egg, the fish sauce and the ground white pepper. Mix thoroughly. Put a scant 1 tsp/5ml of the mixture on each piece of toast. Mix the remaining egg with the milk or water, and brush each pork toast with this. Heat the oil and deep-fry, a few at a time, for 2-3 minutes until browned. Drain on paper towels, arrange on a large plate, and garnish with coriander leaves, cucumber, chilli, or a mixture of all pierced with a toothpick. This recipe makes 20 toasts.

This could be served with the *A Jad* sauce (p. 164).

GOLD BAGS
Tung Tong

4oz/120g minced/ground pork
2 water chestnuts, chopped
1 garlic clove, very finely chopped
ground white pepper
12 small wan ton wrappers
(about 3 × 3in/7.5 × 7.5cm)
oil for deep frying
Sauce:
4 tbs/60ml sugar
4 tbs/60ml rice vinegar
¼ tsp/1.25ml salt
1 small red chilli, cut into fine rings
1 small green chilli, cut into fine rings

Thoroughly mix the pork, garlic, water chestnut and a sprinkling of pepper. Put 1 tsp/5ml of the mixture in the middle of each wrapper, gather up the corners and squash together to make a small bag. When you have your 12 little bags, heat the oil, and deep-fry until they are crisp and dark gold.

Make the sauce. In a small saucepan, dissolve the sugar in the vinegar and boil rapidly, stirring, for about 10 minutes until you have a pale gold syrup. It will thicken as it cools. Add the salt and the sliced chillies, and stir to mix. To eat, the bags are dipped in the sauce.

THAI FRUIT

More varieties of oriental fruit are now appearing in the West but there is often little guidance available as to how they should be handled. Here are a few tips for the most frequently seen of these new arrivals.

Fresh Lychee While the tinned variety is the most common dessert in oriental restaurants, the fresh fruit is still fairly rare, and absolutely wonderful in comparison to its syrupy cousin. Fresh lychees are served in their brittle shells, which are simply cracked open with the fingers and pulled apart to reveal the opalescent fruit within. There is a stone/pit to discard.

Mango There are details on how these should be peeled and set out on p. 168.

Star Fruit (Carambola) This pretty waxy fruit is cut into horizontal slices to preserve its star shape, and eaten with a fork.

Rambutan This is a sort of hairy lychee. To serve, cut it around the middle, remove the top and offer the fruit like an egg in a hairy cup. To eat, the bottom part is held in the fingers and the fruit drawn out with the teeth. There is a seed/pit to discard.

Mangosteen This is considered by some as the queen of fruit. It has a hard dark purple exterior, almost like a shell, with four greenish leaves on top. To get to the fruit, cut the shell all the way around horizontally halfway down with a sharp knife, being careful not to cut into the flesh of the fruit (the shell is usually about ¼in/5mm thick). You can then lift off the top of the shell to find the creamy white segments nestling in the lower half. You should present the fruit already cut, with the cap replaced, so that diners merely have to lift this off and fork out the segments inside. The largest segments will have a seed/pit to discard.

Star fruit, (carambola)

THAI DESSERTS/KONG WAN

MANGO WITH STICKY RICE
Khao Niew Mamuang

This is the best-known of all Thai sweets yet it is also the least typical, being neither a 'liquid' syrup nor a 'dry' cake. There are several varieties of mango, but the very sweetest are best served in this way so as to balance their rich taste. This is clearly a combination of flavours that approaches that perfect balance we aspire to, for no matter how often it is served one never seems to tire of it.

8fl oz/250ml/1 cup thick coconut milk
2 tbs/30ml sugar
½ tsp/2.5ml salt
10oz/300g sticky rice (p. 138) cooked, still warm
3 large ripe mangoes
2 tbs/30ml coconut cream
Serves 3

In a bowl, mix the coconut milk, sugar and salt and stir until the sugar has dissolved. Mix in the still warm cooked rice, and set aside for 30 minutes. Peel the mangoes, and slice the two outside 'cheeks' of each fruit as close to the central stone/pit as possible. Discard the stone. Slice each piece of fruit into 4 pieces lengthways. Mound the rice in the centre of a serving dish and arrange the slices of mango around it. Pour the coconut cream over the rice and serve.

LIQUID DESSERTS

BANANAS IN SYRUP
Kruay Chu'am

There are many varieties of Thai banana, each with subtle variations of flavour. The stubby finger-like banana (sometimes called 'lady's fingers' or apple banana) is very sweet and there is no equivalent outside the tropics. The long dessert banana, which is usually available in the West, has been ripened in storage and has a poor flavour by comparison. These 'cooked' dishes are probably the best way to serve them.

4 oz/120g sugar
8fl oz/250ml/1cup water
4 bananas
4fl oz/125ml/½ cup coconut cream (optional)
¼ tsp/1.25ml salt (optional)

In a small saucepan, dissolve the sugar in the water over a low heat. Strain the mixture through muslin into a larger pan.

Peel the bananas and chop into 2in/5cm pieces. Add to the sugar mixture. Bring to the boil, uncovered, then lower the heat and cook gently, sprinkling with a little cold water 2-3 times. Remove any scum that forms. When the bananas are bright and clear, and the sugar syrup forms threads when lifted with a wooden spoon, turn onto a serving plate. Serve hot, either just as it is, or with the optional coconut cream, slightly salted.

BANANAS IN COCONUT MILK
Kruay Bua Chee

6 bananas
12fl oz/375ml/1½cups coconut milk
2 tbs/30ml granulated sugar
½ tsp/2.5ml salt

Peel the bananas and chop into 2in/5cm segments.

In a saucepan, heat the coconut milk with the sugar and salt, and cook gently until the sugar dissolves. Add the banana pieces and cook gently for 5 minutes.

Divide the mixture into 6-8 small bowls and serve warm.

ORANGES IN SYRUP
Som Loy Geow

This is a hot weather dessert, and you can serve it over ice-cubes to make it really cold.

4 oranges
8oz/225g sugar
12fl oz/375ml/1½cups water
1tsp/5ml rosewater

Peel and segment the oranges, ensuring that no pips/pits, pith or skin remain. Put the segments in a glass dish and set aside.

Sweet sticky rice, beloved of children

In a small saucepan, bring the sugar and water gently to the boil, stirring occasionally. Boil for 15 minutes, until it is the consistency of a thin syrup. Add the rosewater and stir to blend.

Pour the syrup over the orange segments and chill until required.

DRY DESSERTS

The following six recipes are for 'dry' desserts. Some require a little skill in the dipping or turning but their unusual appearance makes this worth the effort.

GOLDEN THREADS
Foy Tong

1 lb/450g sugar
16fl oz/475ml water/2cups water
6 eggs

Make a syrup with the sugar and water. Have a warmed serving dish ready.

Separate the eggs; put the whites aside for another purpose (to make the Sangkaya (p. 172), for example). Place a piece of muslin over a small bowl and strain the egg yolks through it. Beat them lightly.

Prepare either an icing bag with a small nozzle, or a cone made of a double thickness of foil or paper with the hole in the end about $\frac{1}{10}$in/2mm in diameter. In Thailand a banana leaf cone is traditionally used.

Bring the sugar syrup to a simmer. Pour the egg yolks into your icing bag or cone, a little at a time, and carefully trickle and swirl the egg yolks into the syrup, making a spiral about $1\frac{1}{2}$-2in/4-5cm in diameter with a small hole in the middle. Make the spirals one at a time. Cook in the syrup until set – about 2 minutes – and remove by inserting the skewer or chopstick in the hole in the middle of the swirl and lifting it out. Put the swirls on a plate. They will keep for several days.

The author buying oranges outside a temple in Chiang Mai

COCONUT CUSTARD
Sangkaya

While this custard can be made in a bowl, you can really impress your guests by baking it inside a small hollowed out pumpkin or squash, or young coconut. It can be served with sticky rice, if wished.

8fl oz/250ml/1cup thick coconut milk
1 tsp/5ml rosewater
8oz/240g/1cup sugar
½ tsp/2.5ml salt
3 eggs, lightly beaten (use whites only, if you have some to use up)

Dissolve the sugar in the coconut milk, add the rosewater and salt and stir. Add the eggs (or beaten egg whites) and mix well.

Pour the resulting custard into a bowl or a scooped out pumpkin, squash shell, or young coconut. Put in the top of a preheated steamer and cook for 30 minutes, or until set.

Previous pages: Thai desserts: Mango with sticky rice; Met Kanoon (Jackfruit seeds); golden threads; coconut custard steamed in a pumpkin; oranges in syrup

BAKED MOONG BEAN AND COCONUT CUSTARD
Kanom Maw Geang

My family's favourite dessert from Petchaburi; the oddly named 'Sweet curry in a pot'.

14oz/420g (1 packet) split moong beans (available from oriental and Indian stores)
16fl oz/475ml/2cups thick coconut milk (or 1 can)
3 eggs, lightly beaten
1 lb/450g sugar
½ tsp/2.5ml salt
2 tbs/30ml oil
4 shallots, finely sliced

Rinse the moong beans in cold water. Put in a saucepan and cover with about 2in/5cm water. Cook gently for about 30-45 minutes until the beans are completely soft. Drain off any excess water and mash the beans to a smooth paste. Stir in the coconut milk, eggs, sugar and salt. Pour the mixture into a shallow greased pan, about 9 × 9 × 2in/23 × 23 × 5cm, and bake in a medium oven for about 1 hour, until it is golden brown on top and quite firm when pressed lightly.

While the pudding is baking, heat the oil and fry the sliced shallots until dark golden brown; drain on paper towels and set aside.

About 10 minutes before you take the pudding from the oven, preheat the grill/broiler. When it is cooked, put the pudding under the grill/broiler to crisp the top – about 5 minutes. Leave to cool. Sprinkle the fried shallots over the top, cut into small squares (1-1½in/2.5-4cm) and serve.

JACKFRUIT SEEDS
Met Kanoon

These sweetmeats resemble the seeds/pits of the jackfruit, which are like large kidney beans. They are the nearest the amateur can get to making Look Choob.

8oz/230g split moong beans (available from oriental and Indian stores)
6oz/180g desiccated coconut
2 egg yolks, beaten
8oz/240g sugar
12fl oz/375ml/1½ cups water

Rinse the moong beans, place in a small saucepan and cover with 1½in/4cm water. Cook over a medium heat until completely soft – about 30-45 minutes. Drain off any excess water and mash thoroughly. Add the desiccated coconut and mix thoroughly to form a firm paste. Turn the mixture onto a board, and taking pieces about the size of a small walnut, form into small egg shapes.

Make a syrup from the sugar and water and keep it hot. Dip the 'eggs' into the beaten egg yolks and then drop them into the syrup where they should cook briefly. Remove with a small strainer and set them aside to cool. Serve as sweets or candies.

SAGO AND SWEETCORN PUDDING
Saku Khao Pohd

1pt/570ml/2½cups water
2tsp/30ml rosewater
4oz/120g sago or tapioca
¼tsp/1.25ml salt
4oz/120g sugar
6oz/180g sweetcorn kernels, canned or frozen
4oz/120g lotus seeds (available in cans from oriental stores)
4fl oz/125ml/½ cup coconut cream

In a medium saucepan, bring the water to the boil. Add the rosewater, sago or tapioca and salt, stir, and cook until the grains have fully swelled and are cooked through – about 15 minutes. Add the sugar, stir and cook until the sugar is dissolved. Stir in the sweetcorn and then the lotus seeds.

Divide the pudding into 6-8 small bowls, top each one with a spoonful of coconut cream, and serve warm.

TARO CONSERVE
Puak Goan

1 large taro (p. 39), about 2 lbs/1 kg
8oz/230g sugar
8fl oz/250ml/1cup coconut milk

Peel the taro and cut into 1-1½in/2.5-4cm square chunks. Boil or steam them for 15-20 minutes until tender, then drain and mash well.

Dissolve the sugar in the coconut milk over a gentle heat and add it gradually, a few spoonfuls at a time, to the mashed taro. Mix thoroughly. Sieve this mixture into a saucepan and stir over a medium heat until you can form a soft ball with it. (This is to get rid of excess moisture.)

Spread the mixture in a shallow baking tin, about 8in/20cm square, and allow to cool. Cut into small squares and serve with fruit.

Coconuts and bananas

VEGETABLE CARVING

Visitors to my country are often astonished – and sometimes deceived – by the elaborate ways in which the humble carrot or onion can be transformed into delicate flowers. I am not an expert at this art myself, but still endeavour to make a dish as attractive-looking as possible by the addition of a chilli flower or spring onion/scallion tassel.

The following are simple decorative forms which can be achieved quite easily. It is essential, however, to use a small finely-bladed and very sharp knife – a long-bladed craftwork scalpel would do very well.

Carved vegetables: carrot, tomato, red cabbage, cucumber, spring onion

Spring onion/scallion chrysanthemum Cut the white root end of a large spring onion/scallion to a length of approximately 2in/5cm. Keep the leafy end to make the spring onion tassle. Trim off the roots, but cut off as little of the solid root end as possible. Hold the base firmly in a vertical position and, with a very fine blade, make at least ten vertical parallel cuts from tip to base to within approximately ¼in/5mm of the base, making sure you do not cut right through at the bottom. With the thumb and forefinger gently ease out the resulting 'petals' to start to make a flower form. Drop it head down into a bowl of iced water for a few minutes, where the flower will blossom.

Spring onion/scallion tassel Trim the top green end of a spring onion and cut a piece between 2-3in/5-7.5cm long, including a ½in/1cm of the white base. With a very fine blade, or a needle, and holding the white part of the scallion as a base, shred the green part as finely as possible. Drop into a bowl of iced water. The fine shreds will curl back.

Two spring onion (scallion) flowers

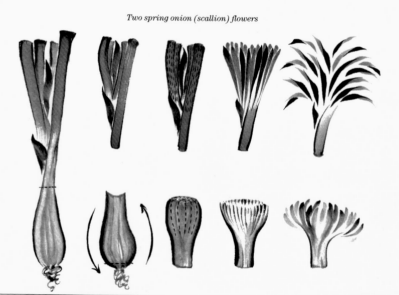

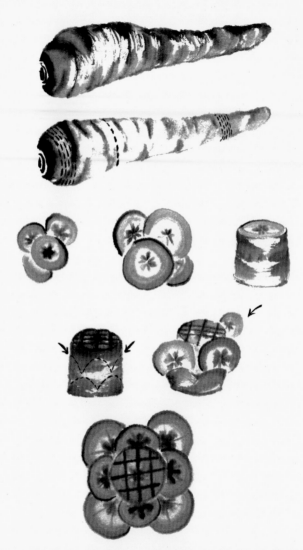

Carrot flower Trim a straight piece of carrot into a 1¾in/4.5cm length. With a sharp blade, carefully slice off 8 rounds, 4 from the fat end and 4 from the narrow end as thin as possible, and set aside. About half-way up the remaining piece of carrot, make 4 incisions ¼in/5mm deep, cutting with a downward motion at equal distances around the circumference. Turn the piece of carrot through 45 degrees and make 4 similar incisions about ¼-½in/5mm-1cm above the first. Take the four largest slices of carrot and insert one into each of the 4 lower incisions. Take the remaining 4 slices and insert into the upper 4 incisions. Cut a cross-hatch of grooves on the top. Put upside down into a bowl of iced water until required.

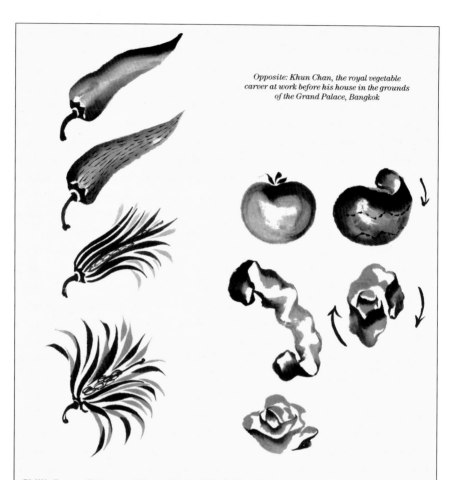

Opposite: Khun Chan, the royal vegetable carver at work before his house in the grounds of the Grand Palace, Bangkok

Chilli flower Take a well-formed red chilli with stem intact 2-3in/5-7.5cm long. Hold the chilli upright in one hand, stem downwards, and, with a very sharp fine blade, cut from tip to stem, without cutting through the stem, at equal distances all the way around. The incisions should not be too deep so that the inside seeds are left intact. Gently pull the strips apart and drop the 'flower' into a bowl of iced water. The strips will curl back from the seed 'stamens'.

Tomato rose Take a well-formed medium-size tomato. With a very sharp blade, working horizontally around the tomato from top to bottom, carefully peel the skin from the tomato as thinly as possible making the edges of the peel wavy, and in one single piece. The strip of peel should be approximately ½in/1cm wide. When you have your strip of peel, curl it around itself (it will tend to do that anyway) as firmly as possible to make a 'rose' shape, gently teasing the upper edges outwards with the thumb and forefinger. In the last but one layer of 'petal' make a vertical notch in the peel so the final ½in/1cm can be slotted in to keep the form in place.

EATING OUT

A PERSONAL CHOICE OF
SOME OF THAILAND'S MANY RESTAURANTS
WITH A SELECTION OF RECIPES

 id-day and three men in spotless white shirts and dark ties are discussing something serious while dipping into bowls of curried noodles. Their sober dress and way of talking marks them out as government officials from one of the nearby ministries. Beyond the restaurant windows in the wide circus is Democracy Monument, a curious mix of Thai traditional forms and European monumental sculpture in the pre-war heroic style. The friezes represent all aspects of Thai life from the military to peasant farmers and they celebrate the country's first constitution following the abrogation of the absolute monarchy in 1932. The monument stands on an island surrounded by circling traffic at the centre of Rajadamnern Avenue or 'the Royal Way of Walking', one of the city's first major highways, built by King Chulalongkorn to link the old, uncomfortable Grand Palace with his new home, the Vimanmek. This broad boulevard was very popular with his children who used it to satisfy the turn of the century passion for cycling. There are photographs of it in 1908 with a Royal motor procession chugging its length. Such events were apparently very popular which makes me want to weep when I think of the appalling traffic today. After the creation of the constitutional monarchy the avenue was lined with government buildings in Thirties functional style to house the burgeoning bureaucracy. The Vijit restaurant near the monument caters for today's functionaries who occupy these rather forbidding edifices. Decorated in subfusc browns it shows a haughty disdain for fashion, the decor being distinctly secondary to the quality of the food. Its customers may not be rich but they do know what good cooking in the Bangkok style is and here they get it. There are no tourists. Vijit is on no one's itinerary, just characters typical of the capital. A fat Chinese businessman moans and complains to a friend about some permit he has failed to obtain that morning all the while placating his distress with large helpings of steamed fish. A young man stares at his fiancée who, with the politeness traditionally expected of young Thai girls, merely nibbles at the food before her no matter how hungry she may really be. If the boyfriend thinks this charming abstinence will last after they are married he need only look at the three women at the table beside him to be disabused. Here are three real Thai civil servants, comfortable of girth and with the major task of the day before them – lunch. They only speak in the interludes when more rice is ladled out. Of course they have good reason, this is a moment to look forward to in a rather dull day and the food is very good indeed and nicely presented without too much fuss, in other words a real city brasserie. Bustling waiters in white shirts and black bow ties complete the picture.

Ever since I opened my own restaurant, eating out has meant something different for me. For one thing, I am always checking up on how other people do it. But more than that, I am always keen to try something new and to work out how I can serve it up myself. All Thai cooks do this and our main source of inspiration remains that marvellous, anonymous legion serving up food on the streets and in the markets of my country. But of course there are also wonderful restaurants like Vijit and I thought it would be useful if on my last visit to Thailand I went round some of the restaurants that I have enjoyed to pass on the atmosphere that makes me appreciate them so much and to make up a selection of recipes based on what these restaurants have to offer. I have not picked these restaurants because they are the 'top ten' centres of gourmet life in South East Asia, but rather because each offers a different experience: some, great food; others, entertainment. The recipes that follow are my own versions of what I have eaten, adapted to suit the ordinary kitchen, a chance to create something a little more spectacular than usual but nevertheless still

Democracy Monument, Bangkok – Vijit restaurant is to the right

within the bounds of the possible. If you do visit Thailand, I hope you will look up some of the places I mention and enjoy them as much as I have.

Across town, near my family house, is Ton Kruang, a restaurant in one of the surviving 'colonial houses' by what was the Sathorn Klong, now an expressway. Here you find an altogether different crowd from Vijit, younger and certainly more fashionable, the sort of people who work in the nearby business district around Silom Road, the banks and finance houses, the airlines and international hotels. These young people are the principal beneficiaries of my country's recent economic boom. They wear the latest fashions, nowadays produced by our own designers, they read magazines that show styles in interior decoration, offer new recipes and suggest interesting places for dining out. The Thai word for what these people are seeking is *Sa-mart* which may sound a little like *Sanuk* but is really only our version of the English word, smart, meaning well-presented or clever. The Sa-mart crowd are always on the lookout for somewhere new to eat and Bangkok boasts many outposts of almost every cuisine: Italian pizzeria, French nouvelle cuisine, German beer huts and of course our own Chinatown with some of the finest Chinese restaurants in Asia. Recently, in the wake of the Japanese economic miracle we have acquired innumerable Sushi bars. But to most Thais all these are just exotic amusements to be tried occasionally.

As far as Thai restaurants are concerned, many come and go with astonishing speed. Because our food is so good at home, restaurants have to offer something more and that means entertainment, usually music or interesting decor. If a new restaurant offers these along will come the Sa-mart crowd for a while but then they will move on to something new and the restaurant will wither and die. Just a few manage to go on being fashionable and my own favourite is Moon Shadow because it both looks pretty yet you can eat well. The restaurant is a long

Fast food Thai style

Signs of Bangkok's notorious nightlife

narrow traditional Thai room all the more surprising for being situated in a rather nondescript modern square in Gaysorn, a faded shopping district. The owner has filled the dark wooden room with his own collection of antiques, a clutter of beautiful things. Especially memorable are the old gilded Chinese shop signs, their black lacquered backgrounds embossed or carved with vivid golden characters. This is basically a seafood restaurant but after the main courses you can vary this by crossing to Moon Shadow's sister restaurant, Sometime, where there are ice-creams and desserts served in two little rooms cluttered with European and Oriental bric-a-brac – an Austrian Arts and Crafts clock, a Deco lamp, a Bell Epoque print of the Thai Royal Family – a complete jumble and all for sale, even the chairs you are sitting on!

Away from the Sa-mart set a more traditional Thai evening on the town is usually an all-male affair. Groups of colleagues go on from work to a restaurant taking their own drink with them. Scotch whisky or French brandy if they are well off. Thai Mekong 'whisky' if not. The waiters will constantly replenish the glasses with much watered drink. Dish after dish will be brought and sampled, often very chilli-hot to stimulate the drinking. Conversation will get more and more animated and the cares of the day will recede. Today, such an evening would probably end with nothing hotter than a bowl of noodles but in the past there might have been a visit to one of the city's massage parlours. There has always been a Thai tradition of massage, at its most refined it is a form of medicine practised within temple precincts, but in the past even as pure entertainment it was more of a geisha-like activity than the raw prostitution it became when the Americans seized on Bangkok as their main Rest and Recreation centre during the Vietnam War. Countless girls left the impoverished north east to end up in the massage parlours and Go-Go bars of the capital and after the troops came the tourists. Modern fears are beginning to

cause this tide to recede and the notorious Patpong Road area is becoming just another half-hour on the tourist itinerary, a place to be photographed in front of the sleazy neon signs. We are very relaxed about these matters and only get irritated when Western newspapers accuse us of running the sex capital of the world – who, we ask, created the problem in the first place? Today, most young Thais, unlike that earlier generation, shun the dim lighting and plush decor of the parlours and are more likely to spend their evenings in one of the sensational discos offering sound and light displays with vast moving sets that turn the cavernous rooms into pieces of spectacular theatre. But whether it is Patpong or disco all sides come together when the show is over and it is time for a midnight snack. Then it is back to the market, as I've said, the best restaurant of all, undecorated, unfashionable, always open.

Most of our cooks come from the market tradition, and few have any other formal training yet some have proved to be astute business people who have gone far from their original stall by the roadside and none more so than a woman called Som Jai. Her story has some similarities with that of Ba Yon in Chiang Mai – Som Jai's husband also worked in a pork abbatoir and she too cooked and sold her food to make a little extra for the family. Her speciality was *Tod Man* the spicy fish cakes served with a cucumber and nut pickle. She and her husband would rise at five in the morning, he would go to market for her while she began cooking. They might have gone on living like that, as indeed thousands do, but something told Som Jai that luck was with her and this was confirmed during the Second World War when a piece of shrapnel set fire to the little food shop she had set up; and, rushing to save her child, she knocked over a pot of curry on the stove which miraculously extinguished the flames. Clearly, cooking would bring her good fortune. Indeed, the passion for her *Tod Man* spread and although lacking formal education Som Jai was able to save

Khun Som Jai, founder of the D'Jit Pochana restaurant chain

Previous pages: Tumnak Thai, the world's biggest restaurant

her earnings and open a restaurant. Her business flourished and grew until today she owns the most successful chain of Thai restaurants in the world. Named after her husband, the D'Jit Pochana group has several branches in Bangkok with a restaurant in Los Angeles and a new one planned for Singapore. She was able to send her children to study business methods abroad and they now run the company, but it was all her work originally. The D'Jit Pochana restaurants are unspectacular yet reliable, they cater for Thai families who know what they want and know they will find it there. The decor is safe and middle-class – swagged curtains, fitted carpets, modernish chairs, but they still sell the best *Tod Man* going. Som Jai is now an old lady and a very successful one and is understandably grateful for that opportune pot of curry.

Of course most market cooks remain just that, though they are not as anonymous as they may appear to the outside. The *Thai Shell: Good Food Guide* has an astonishing out-reach and includes not only well established restaurants but also quite small market-stalls. It must have a stunning number of correspondents. Unfortunately for the visitor, the guide is only published in Thai but you can look out for the 'Shell Recommended' symbol, a rice bowl with blue lettering. There is one such place, an otherwise nondescript wooden room with a simple cooking range and glass fronted storage cabinet near Pratu Muang Chiang Mai, the Old City Gate in Chiang Mai, but it bears the Shell symbol and is justifiably famous for its *Kow Man Gai*, an apparently simple dish of boiled chicken with rice cooked in the resultant stock, but one very difficult to get just right. Also important is the side sauce of yellow soya bean and ginger. So influential is the guide that those not in it have been known to put up a sign "Not yet visited by Shell". To get into the guide a place must serve first rate food, though little consideration is given to the decor or the cleanliness of the place – the best restaurant in Chiang Mai, Aroon Rai is frankly scruffy with cobwebs wrapped round the rows of old whisky bottles and with plastic topped tables that show evidence of the last time they were wiped. Nobody cares because the place serves up the best northern food and no punches pulled with the chillies. The visitor who feels that there are limits to this sort of adventure will be better off at Baan Suan, literally House and Garden, and exactly that – a traditional northern teak stilt house set in pretty grounds on the outskirts of the town. Here you can still taste that authentic Thai/Burmese food but under smarter and therefore more expensive conditions.

In Hua Hin the restaurants near the harbour combine good food with beautiful surroundings without any effort, being set on stilts above the water with charming views of the fishing boats bobbing at the jetty. For me, the best is the middle restaurant, the Sang Thai. Indeed I think it serves some of the best seafood in the country. The owner has gone on to become a successful entrepreneur in the construction industry but keeps up the restaurant because it brought him his first

success and he has no wish to break this good fortune. Perhaps because of that the restaurant is run with great care and the selection of fish and seafood on the stall at the entrance is especially well-chosen. The owner has good contacts who tell him where the best fish can be found and if the fishermen of Hua Hin don't have a good catch he sends his drivers further along the coast to find better.

For a comparable choice in Bangkok you would have to go to the Seafood Market in Sukhumvit Road. Although the cooking is nowhere near as good as that of the Sang Thai the sheer abundance of the seafood is a spectacle that attracts large crowds. The restaurant is aptly named for this is no discreet room with carefully dimmed lighting but a hangar-like space, overbright with neon striplights: a supermarket. Although this may not be everyone's idea of where to go for an evening out there are compensations. It is great fun. Above the entrance a huge lobster in scarlet neon indicates the way in, down a driveway lined with batteries of cooks in white chef's hats, all frantically chopping and stir-frying and ladling out lobsters and crabs and dishes of clams as if they were on a mass-production line in a factory – which in a way they are. You pass through a channel in this mad activity to enter the supermarket. A head waiter hands you over to an underling who guides you through row upon row of tables to your own place. You settle your things and then you are ready to join the chain gang. Having grabbed a supermarket trolley you set off down the counter that runs the entire length of the hall on which is displayed everything imaginable from the seas around Thailand – Phuket lobsters, oysters from the Eastern gulf, great piles of huge red snapper, writhing tanks of eels – you pick what you fancy and go on to collect any vegetables and salads you wish. Having passed the cashier you push your trolley to your table where your waiter will note down how you want your haul cooked. They will do it almost any way you choose: sole meuniere, that's fine; Chinese-style fish steamed with ginger and spring onions; or Thai style deep-fried and smothered in chilli and garlic: it's up to you. Although it all sounds a bit mechanical it is in fact very entertaining and easy to cope with which explains the crowds of tourists that come to enjoy the spectacle – and that is of course what the place is all about. It is theatre rather than great cooking and that is something a lot of new restaurants in Bangkok now specialize in. To satisfy the Thai love of novelty a virtual city of restaurants has opened in the area of Ruchadapisek Road in the north of the city. Each is a complex of Thai style buildings offering a vast range of food and each lays on some particular attraction to draw attention to itself. There are enormous car-parks as it is necessary to drive out to these places and there are dozens of whistle-blowing car-hops to find you a space. A bevvy of pretty girls in traditional dress is lined up at the entrance to say *Sawasdi*, or welcome, hands together, heads bowed, as you go in. After that it is up to you to decide

Opposite:
Traditional theatre
from a mural in the
Marble Temple,
Bangkok

where and what you want to eat from the choices available. At Bua Tong you are offered a selection of stilt houses built round an artificial lake on which noodle boats and sweetmeat-sellers ply their trade. It is strange to realize that most of the customers are young professional Bangkokians whose ideal home is a modern villa with a car-port, yet who choose to eat in a sort of Disneyland version of Old Siam. In the lake the waters boil with writhing masses of shark-headed fish that thrash and leap to get at the scraps thrown by diners. Needless to say, children love it. However, I prefer its neighbour, Tumnak Thai, which as well as serving food from every region of Thailand, also has the distinction of being the largest restaurant in the world according to the *Guinness Book of Records*. It is so spread out the waiters whizz around on roller skates which is noisy but exhilarating to watch.

Despite many changes brought about by the breathtaking modernization of the last ten years it is still difficult to eat badly in Thailand and now that the necessary ingredients are being exported it is possible to enjoy the same high quality abroad. I have had wonderful meals in The Siamese Princess in Los Angeles and friends have told me of other authentic places there and in Chicago and New York. The Thai food phenomenon is only just beginning in France where the main Oriental connection remains Vietnam, but I am sure it cannot be long before the mania for our food spreads beyond the Anglo-Saxon world to Europe. My own restaurant, the Chiang Mai in Soho, was the first to bring regional Thai cooking to London and I hope to open a real Thai seafood restaurant in the near future as there is something about Thai cooking and water, whether the sea or the river, that seems to make the perfect combination. In fact, in thinking of which restaurant I would mention last in this book, I had no doubt that it should be one close to the Chao Phya, the great river running through Bangkok.

Which restaurant to recommend was a problem as there are many choices. The Oriental Hotel, reputedly the country's finest, maintains a launch, the *Oriental Queen*, that journeys upriver between central Bangkok and our ancient ruined capital of Ayuthaya. It offers a renowned buffet meal en route. But if you don't want to travel there is the Rim Nam, a Thai wooden building on the opposite bank to the hotel that serves true Thai food without pressing too hard on the chilli pedal. In fact there are dozens of candidates all along the river-front but somehow none seemed to have that something extra I wanted. But then, on my last visit, my sister and her husband resolved the problem by taking me to Bua. I thought this was going to be just another of those huge restaurant complexes like Tumnak Thai, but Bua turned out to have something different: a two-tiered boat set with tables where we dined and sailed at the same time. But the thing that made this special was that our journey was not through the smart centre of Bangkok with its sky-scraper hotels and elegant palaces, but down-river near

Rice barges heading back up the Chao Phya at night

Klong Tuey, the country's main working harbour. As we ate, we drifted past huge tankers riding at anchor with what looked like only a single lonely watchman to guard them. As we settled to a meal of fish and duck we passed power stations belching smoke, cranes silhouetted against the fading light, a rusty old cargo boat suddenly lit up by the sparks of welder working on her bows. Even at night there was bustle and energy as lorries came and went around the long open rice warehouses, their white mountains ghostly under arclights. This was the real river, and as we returned to our mooring I saw three rice barges riding high in the water returning to the inland paddies. On board, the boatman and his family were gathered round their cooking fire enjoying their evening meal. I wished them well and now end this story where it began, with an image from the cycle of that small white grain that nourishes the East and for which we should always be thankful.

Gratong Tong, *golden baskets*

The following recipes are my own versions of the dishes I have sampled in the restaurants I selected. Some are quite simple adaptations, suitable for the home kitchen, and are not the original recipes of the master-chefs whose creations I have enjoyed.

GOLDEN BASKETS
Gratong Tong

To make these batter cases you will need a special Thai implement which looks like a fluted fairy cake tin at the end of a long handle (in the US you could use a timbale iron). But a small ladle (bowl approximately 2in/5cm diameter) would make a reasonable substitute.

Batter:
8oz/230g flour
½ tsp/2.5ml salt
1 egg
8fl oz/250ml/1cup water
oil for deep frying

Put the flour and salt in a bowl and mix. Break the egg into the flour and mix. Gradually add the water, stirring or whisking constantly until thoroughly blended. You should have a thick creamy batter. Allow to rest for an hour. Heat the oil. Dip the chosen implement into the hot oil to heat both inside and outside surfaces thoroughly. Then dip the outside of the hot mould into the batter, making sure that only the *outside* surface is covered with batter – *not* the inside. Put the batter-covered mould immediately into the hot oil where, after about 20 seconds, the case should be cooked enough to detach itself from the mould or spoon. Remove the mould and continue to fry the case until it is golden brown. Remove the case from the deep-fryer with a strainer or slotted spoon, and drain on kitchen towels. The cases should be thin and crisp. Repeat the process until the batter is finished (the amount given should produce about 20 cases). At this point the cases, drained and dry, may be stored in a sealed container until required, though they should not be kept for longer than a week.

Filling for Golden Baskets:
4 tbs/60ml oil
3 garlic cloves, finely chopped
8oz/230g minced/ground chicken
2 carrots, cleaned and finely diced
1 onion, finely chopped
½ potato, finely chopped
½ tsp/2.5ml ground white pepper
½ tsp/2.5ml ground turmeric
2 tsp/10ml curry powder
1 tbs/15ml sugar
2 tbs/30ml light soy sauce
½ tsp/2.5ml salt
coriander leaves, to garnish

In a wok or frying pan/skillet, heat the oil until a light haze appears. Add the garlic and fry until golden brown. Add the minced chicken, stir thoroughly and cook until the meat starts to become opaque. Add the diced carrot, onion and potato, mix and stir thoroughly and cook for 20 seconds or so. Add the white pepper, turmeric and curry powder. Stir and cook for another 20 seconds. Add the sugar, soy sauce and salt and stir the mixture thoroughly.

Allow the mixture to cool before filling the batter cases. Garnish each filled case with coriander leaves and serve.

Opposite: Beef with crispy basil and wing bean salad

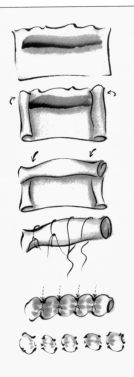

Stuffing and cutting bean curd sheets with crab

BEAN CURD SHEET STUFFED WITH CRAB

Hoi Joh

Hoi Joh are not easy to make but have a wonderfully delicate flavour.

4-5 bean curd sheets (p. 37), about 6 × 12in/15 × 30cm
6oz/180g crabmeat
2oz/60g minced/ground pork
2 garlic cloves, finely chopped
1 egg
1 tbs/15ml light soy sauce
½ tsp/2.5ml ground white pepper
1 tsp/5ml sugar
pinch of salt
oil for deep frying
lettuce and sliced cucumber, to garnish
Sauce:
1 small preserved plum (available in jars)
6 tbs/90ml vinegar
4 tbs/60ml sugar

Soak the bean curd sheets in cold water for about 5-6 minutes until soft and pliable. Thoroughly combine the crabmeat, pork, garlic, egg, soy sauce, pepper, sugar and salt. Divide the mixture into 4 portions. Put one portion of the crab mixture onto half a bean curd sheet (handle carefully as they tend to split, but don't worry if they do as you can 'patch' any holes). Shape the mixture into a sausage, then wrap the sheet around the meat, folding in the ends. You should have 4 wrapped sausages about 6ins/15cm long. Tie with cotton thread to divide into 4-5 sections. Steam the packages for about 10 minutes.

Remove from the steamer and allow to cool. At this point the method may be stopped, and the packages set aside for final cooking later that day, or even the following day (they can also be frozen at this stage).

To finish, cut the packages where they are tied with cotton and remove the thread. You will now have 5-6 roughly ball-shaped pieces from each. Heat the oil and deep-fry the pieces until golden brown. Make the sauce. Boil all the ingredients together, stirring, until the sugar has dissolved. Check for flavour – the sauce should be sweet and sour. Serve the deep-fried balls with the sauce, garnished with lettuce and cucumber.

FISH SOUP WITH TAMARIND AND GINGER

Pla Dom Som

12oz/340g fish fillet (eg. cod, coley or monkfish)
1 shallot, chopped
1 garlic clove, chopped
1 tsp/5ml shrimp paste
1 coriander root, chopped
shaking of ground white pepper
2 tbs/30ml oil
1pt/570ml/2½cups chicken stock/broth
1 tsp/5ml finely slivered ginger
2 tbs/30ml fish sauce
2 tsp/5ml sugar
1 tbs/15ml tamarind juice, or 2 tbs/30ml lemon juice
2 spring onions/scallions, finely sliced into 1½in/4cm lengths
Serves 4

Skin the fish fillets and cut into 1in/2.5cm cubes. Set aside. With a pestle and mortar or blender, pound or blend the shallot, garlic, shrimp paste, coriander root and pepper to a paste. In a small frying pan/skillet, heat the oil, add the paste and fry quickly for a few seconds. Set aside. In a saucepan, heat the stock, add the fried paste and stir thoroughly to mix. Add the fish, bring to the boil and skim if necessary. Add the ginger, fish sauce, sugar and tamarind (or lemon) juice and simmer together gently for 2-3 minutes to allow the fish to cook through thoroughly. Add the spring onion, and stir. Serve in a tureen or individual bowls.

HOT AND SOUR BAMBOO SALAD
Sup Normai

You will find this described as 'asparagus' on some menus. It is actually young bamboo, and can be bought in jars, marinated with yanang leaf. It is normally only available in Thailand, so if you can't find it, use young, or small bamboo shoots; hold the thick end in one hand, and use a fork to shred the bamboo shoots.

3 tbs/45ml stock/broth
2 tbs/30ml fish sauce
1 tbs/15ml lemon juice
½ tsp/5ml sugar
½-1 tsp/2.5-5ml chilli powder
6oz/180g shredded bamboo shoot
1 tbs/15ml ground browned rice (p. 140)
1 small spring onion/scallion, chopped
4-6 coriander leaves

In a saucepan, heat together the stock, fish sauce, lemon juice, sugar and chilli powder. Bring quickly to the boil, add the shredded bamboo shoot and stir thoroughly. Add the browned rice, stir, and turn onto a serving dish. Garnish with the spring onion and coriander leaves.

WING BEAN SALAD
Yam Tua Proo

The success of this dish depends very much on the very fine slicing of the beans. Substitute stringless beans for wing beans if necessary.

8oz/230g wing beans, cut diagonally into fine slices (⅛in/2mm wide)
6oz/180g boiled chicken, without skin, finely shredded
2 tbs/30ml coconut cream
2 tbs/30ml oil
3 garlic cloves, finely chopped
3 shallots, finely sliced
1 tsp/5ml crushed dried red chilli
1½ tbs/22.5ml nam prik pow (Tom Yam sauce, p. 80)
2 tbs/30ml ground roasted peanuts
2 tbs/30ml lemon juice
2 tbs/30ml fish sauce
1 tsp/5ml sugar
2 tbs/30ml stock/broth

Boil a pan of water. Put the beans in a wire sieve, dip into the water for a few seconds to

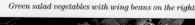
Green salad vegetables with wing beans on the right

blanch and set aside. Have the shredded chicken ready and set aside. Gently heat the coconut cream in a small pan until it thickens slightly, stirring from time to time. In a small frying pan/skillet, heat the oil, add the garlic and fry until golden brown. Remove with a slotted spoon and set aside. Add the shallot to the oil and fry until golden brown and crisp. Remove and set aside. Next briefly fry the crushed dried chilli, remove and set aside. In a bowl, mix the *Nam prik pow* with the ground peanuts, lemon juice, fish sauce, sugar and stock. Add the fried garlic, shallots and dried chilli. Mix thoroughly. Add the shredded chicken and mix; finally add the beans and mix in gently. All the ingredients should be thoroughly blended. Turn onto a serving dish and spoon the coconut cream over the top.

PAK BUNG IN BLACK BEAN SAUCE
Pad Pak Bung Fidang

In Thailand, the plant used in this recipe is called *Pak Bung* but you would find it in Chinese stores as *Kang Kung*. Its English/American name is the rather unattractive Swamp Cabbage, and it is also sometimes known as Water Convolvulus. If you can't find it under any of these names, spinach may be substituted.

This dish takes less than 1 minute to cook!

2 tbs/30ml oil
1 small garlic clove, finely chopped
2 small chillies, red or green, finely chopped
4oz/120g *Pak Bung*
1 tsp/5ml yellow or black bean sauce
1 tbs/15ml oyster sauce
1 tbs/15ml fish sauce
4 tbs/60ml stock/broth or water
½ tsp/2.5ml sugar

Heat the oil, add the garlic and fry until it starts to brown. Add the chillis and fry. Then quickly add the Pak Bung and stir-fry for 3-4 seconds. Add all the other ingredients and quickly stir-fry together. Serve.

YOUNG CHILLI SPICY SAUCE
Nam Prik Num

In the north of Thailand there are young large fresh chillies, coloured pale green, like leaves. This spicy sauce is based on them, but a reasonable substitute could be made using the large fresh green chillies you can buy in the West, though these will be fully matured and dark green. Aside from the chillies, the unique flavour of this Nam Prik comes from the slight burning of the ingredients, a taste found also in North African cooking. This sauce can be served with a variety of cut vegetables – cucumber, carrot, celery, broccoli – and with prawn crackers or pork crackers.

The Aroon Rai restaurant, Chiang Mai

10 garlic cloves
2 shallots, peeled
4 large green chillies
2 medium tomatoes
5 small green aubergines/eggplant or 1 large aubergine/eggplant, peeled
2 tbs/30ml lemon juice
2 tbs/30ml fish sauce
1 tbs/15ml sugar
1 tbs/15ml chopped spring onion/scallion
1 tbs/15ml chopped coriander leaf

Grill/broil the garlic, shallots, chillies and tomatoes for approximately 10 minutes until slightly charred. While these are cooking, put the aubergines in a small pan, cover with water and boil for 5-10 minutes until tender (the cooking time will be slightly less for one larger aubergine). When all the above are ready, cut the tops off the aubergines and skin the tomato. Place these and the other grilled/broiled ingredients into a mortar or food processor, and pound or process this mixture until well blended, but not too fine. Turn into a bowl and add the remaining ingredients. Taste for balance. It should be quite hot and sharp, but if too hot add a little more sugar and lemon juice and perhaps a little more fish sauce.

Large red chillies, beloved of Thais who like their food burning hot

CURRY NOODLE
Gueyteow Keh

2oz/60g dry *Sen Mee* noodles (p. 85), soaked in cold water for 15 minutes to soften, then drained
4oz/120g beef, cubed
1 hard-boiled/cooked egg
3 tbs/90ml oil
1 block prepared fried bean curd (p. 37), finely sliced
1 shallot, finely sliced
1 garlic clove, finely chopped
2 tsp/10ml Red curry paste (p. 37)
4 tbs/60ml coconut milk
1 tsp/5ml curry powder
1 tbs/15ml fish sauce
1 tsp/5ml sugar
1 tbs/15ml ground roasted peanuts
coriander leaves, to garnish
Serves 2

Set the noodles aside, but have ready a pan of hot water in which to warm them. Put the beef in a small pan and cover with water; boil gently for 10-15 minutes. Cut the egg into quarters and set aside.

In a small frying pan/skillet, heat 1 tbs/15ml oil and fry the sliced bean curd until slightly crisp; drain, and set aside. Reheat the oil (add a little more if necessary) and fry the shallot until dark golden brown and crisp. Set aside in the pan. In a wok or frying pan heat 2 tbs/30ml oil, add the garlic and fry for a few seconds until golden brown. Add the curry paste, stir to mix and cook for a few seconds. Add the coconut milk, stir thoroughly to blend and heat through for a few seconds. With a slotted spoon or strainer, remove the beef from its pan and add to the mixture. Stir to make sure each piece is covered with the curry. Add 2 cups of the water in which the beef has boiled (make up the amount with cold water if necessary), the curry powder, fish sauce and sugar. Stir to mix and cook together for about 5 minutes.

Have two serving bowls ready. Bring the pan of hot water to the boil, put the noodles in a sieve or strainer with a handle and dip into the water for 2-3 seconds to warm through. Drain and divide between the serving bowls. Arrange the quartered egg on top of the noodles. Add the peanuts to the beef curry soup, stir, and pour over the noodles. Garnish with the reserved fried bean curd, fried shallots with a little of their oil, and the coriander.

FRIED PRAWN WITH CHILLI AND LIME LEAF

Chu Chee Gung

2 tbs/30ml oil
2 garlic cloves, finely chopped
1 tbs/15ml Red curry paste (p. 37)
2 tbs/30ml stock/broth or water
6-8 large raw prawns, shelled and deveined
2 tbs/30ml fish sauce
1 tbs/15ml sugar
1 tbs/15ml lemon juice
2 lime leaves, finely slivered
1 long red chilli, finely slivered
Serves 2

In a wok or frying pan, heat the oil, add the garlic and fry until golden brown. Add the curry paste, stir to mix, and cook together for a few seconds. Add the stock and mix thoroughly. Add the prawns and turn in the mixture until coated thoroughly. Cook for a few seconds until the prawns become opaque. Stirring quickly after each addition, add the fish sauce, sugar, lemon juice, lime leaves and chilli. Stir thoroughly for 2-3 seconds and serve. This dish should be quite dry.

WHITE RADISH CAKE

Kanom Pad Ga

1 white radish (mooli) (weighing about 2 lbs/1kg)
6oz/180g/1½cups rice flour
2 tbs/30ml wheat flour
2 tbs/30ml water

Trim and peel the radish and cut into small cubes. Using a food processor or blender, mash the radish as fine as possible. This will have to be done in 2-3 batches. When all is finely ground, mix thoroughly with the rice and wheat flours and the water. Turn the mixture into a shallow tin or heatproof dish, about 8in/20cm square, to a depth of about 1in/2.5cm. Heat up your steamer (or use your

largest saucepan with an upturned bowl in the bottom on which to rest the tin) and steam the cake for about 30 minutes from the time the steamer is hot. If you are using a thicker dish you will have to steam it for a little longer. When an inserted knife comes out clean, remove from the heat, and allow to cool and dry out completely. It will set more solidly as it cools. Cut the cake into rectangles, about 1 × 2in/2.5 × 5cm.

WHITE RADISH CAKE WITH PRAWN

Kanom Pad Ga Gung

The white radish cake can be served in a number of ways but this is one of my favourites and goes well with *Prik nam som* (p. 86).

3 tbs/45ml oil
1 batch white radish cake
2 garlic cloves, finely chopped
4oz/120g peeled prawns
1 egg
2 tbs/30ml fish sauce
1 tsp/5ml dark soy sauce
½ tsp/2.5ml sugar
shaking of ground white pepper
1oz/30g beansprouts, rinsed and drained
3 spring onions/scallions, cut into 1in/2.5cm slivers
Serves 3-4

In a frying pan/skillet, preferably non-stick, heat half the oil. Add half the radish cake pieces and, stirring and turning constantly, fry until they are browned on all sides. Remove from the pan and set aside. Add the rest of the oil and reheat. Add the garlic and fry until golden brown. Add the prawns and quickly stir-fry for 2-3 seconds. Break in the egg, stir to mix and cook for a few seconds until the egg starts to set. Add the reserved fried radish cake and mix thoroughly. Quickly add the fish sauce, soy sauce, sugar, pepper, beansprouts and spring onions. Mix quickly and thorough-

White radish or mooli

ly. By this time the prawns should be heated through and the egg cooked. Turn onto serving dish.

The remaining radish cake can be fried and used with other ingredients.

CLAMS WITH CHILLI AND BASIL
Hoy Lai Pad Nam Prik Pow

| 1 lb/½kg baby clams with shell |
| 2 tbs/30ml oil |
| 2 garlic cloves, finely chopped |
| 1 tbs/15ml chillies in oil (Nam prik pow p. 80) |
| 2 tbs/30ml fish sauce |
| 2 tbs/30ml stock/broth or water |
| ½ tsp/2.5ml sugar |
| 2 long red chillies, finely slivered |
| 20 holy basil leaves |

Rinse the clams under cold water, discarding any which do not close when shaken. Drain and set aside. In a wok or frying pan/skillet, heat the oil, add the garlic and fry until golden brown. Add the clams and the chillies in oil and stir thoroughly. Stirring after each addition, add the remaining ingredients. Cook, continuing to stir, until the clams have opened. Discard any which remain closed. Turn into serving bowl.

OYSTERS WITH RED BEAN CURD
Hoy Nang Lum Dow Hoo Yee Pow

Oysters are rare enough in the West for most people not to want to do too much to them, so this recipe requires more than a little courage as well as not a little expense.

| 6 oysters, opened |
| 2 tbs/30ml oil |
| 1 garlic clove, finely chopped |
| 1 tbs/15ml red bean curd, gently mashed |
| 1 tbs/15ml lemon juice |
| 1 medium-size fresh red or green chilli, finely chopped |
| 1 tsp/5ml sugar |

Arrange the opened oysters in a grill-pan/broiler rack, or on a flameproof serving plate. Pre-heat the grill/broiler. In a frying pan/skillet heat the oil, add the garlic and fry until golden brown. Set aside. In a small bowl, thoroughly mix the mashed red bean curd, lemon juice, chilli and sugar. Spoon the mixture onto the oysters (1 tsp/5ml per oyster) and grill/broil for 3-4 minutes until the oysters become opaque. Pour a little garlic oil on each oyster and serve.

GRILLED LOBSTER WITH GARLIC AND FRESH CHILLI
Gung Yi Pow Kratiem Prik Sot

| 1½-2lb/750g-1kg lobster cooked and halved |
| 4 tbs/60ml oil |
| 2 garlic cloves, finely chopped |
| 1 shallot, finely chopped |
| 2 small red chillies, finely chopped |
| 2 small green chillies, finely chopped |
| 2 tbs/30ml fish sauce |
| 1 tsp/2.5ml sugar |
| *Serves 2* |

Remove the claws from the lobster and set aside to eat separately. Pre-heat the grill/broiler, and lay the two lobster halves ready on a grill-pan/broiler rack. In a small frying pan/skillet, heat the oil, add the garlic, and fry until golden brown. Add the shallot, chillies, fish sauce and sugar and stir-fry quickly for about 10 seconds. Remove from the heat and spoon the mixture over the two lobster halves, loosening the flesh and spreading the mixture as much as possible. Grill/broil for about 3-4 minutes and serve.

FISH WITH LEMON SAUCE
Pla Manow

Fish from northern waters, such as lemon sole, are particularly suitable for this brilliantly simple recipe.

| 1 flat fish, (eg. pomphret, plaice or lemon sole) cleaned, rinsed and patted dry |
| 2 tbs/30ml oil |
| 2 garlic cloves, finely chopped |
| 4 long red chillies, finely chopped |
| 2 tbs/30ml fish sauce |
| 3 tbs/45ml lemon juice |
| 2 tbs/30ml sugar |
| 4 tbs/60ml stock/broth or water |
| 2 tbs/15ml flour |
| coriander leaves, to garnish |

Shallow fry the fish, making sure it is still quite moist. Set aside.

In a frying pan/skillet, heat the oil, add the garlic and lightly fry until golden. Add the chillies, stir to mix and fry for a few seconds. Stirring briskly after each addition, add the fish sauce, lemon juice, sugar and stock or water. Mix the flour with 2 tbs/30ml water and add 1 tsp/5ml at a time (you won't have to use it all) to thicken slightly. Pour over the fish, garnish with coriander leaves and serve.

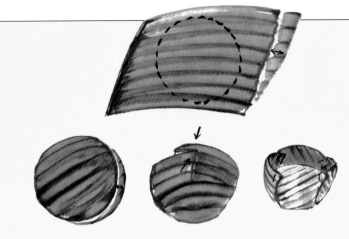

Making banana leaf cups

SPICY PICKLED MUD-FISH
Jow Bong

This is a pungent sauce, much loved in the north-east – an Issan dish. The pickled mud-fish (sometimes cat-fish) is available pre-prepared in small jars, and is very salty. This recipe is used as a dipping sauce for pieces of raw vegetable.

5 shallots
5 garlic cloves
8 small red or green chillies
3 long red or green chillies
1 medium tomato
2 tbs/30ml slivered galangal
1 tbs/15ml pickled mud-fish (available in 8oz/230g jars)
2 tbs/30ml lemon juice
1 tbs/15ml fish sauce
2 tbs/30ml ground dried shrimp

Put the shallots, garlic, chillies, tomato and galangal on a piece of foil and grill/broil until they start to char slightly. With a pestle and mortar or blender, pound or blend them together thoroughly. Add the piece of mud-fish with its liquid and blend. Then add the lemon juice, fish sauce and ground shrimp and mix. Turn into a small bowl and serve with raw vegetables.

Previous pages: Chicken wrapped in bandan leaf, grilled oysters with red bean curd, curried fish steamed in banana leaf, grilled lobster with garlic and fresh chilli

CURRIED FISH STEAMED IN BANANA LEAF
Haw Muk

If possible, you should use banana leaves to make the little cups in which the curried fish is steamed. If you cannot, a small bowl the size of a tea-cup will do.

The filling:
2 heaped tbs/40ml finely chopped Chinese cabbage
6oz/180g cod (or similar fish), pounded
2 tsp/10ml Red curry paste (p. 37)
2 tbs/30ml ground peanuts
1 tbs/15ml lime leaf, finely chopped
1 egg
2 tbs/30ml thick coconut milk
1 tbs/15ml fish sauce
To garnish:
2 tsp/10ml thick coconut cream
1 long red chilli, finely slivered
Serves 2

First make the banana leaf cups. For 2 cups you need 4 pieces of banana leaf, each about 5in/12cm square. Place two pieces, one on top of the other, over an inverted bowl and of about 4in/10cm diameter. Cut around the bowl. Arrange the two rounds of banana leaf so that the dull sides face each other. Make a ½in/1cm tuck about 1½in/4cm deep at any point on the circumference and staple it. Repeat this at the opposite point, and then at the two side points. You will now have a slightly opened squared-off cup.

Place a heaped tablespoon of Chinese cabbage in the bottom of each banana cup, then make the filling. Mix the fish, curry paste, peanuts, lime leaf, egg, coconut milk and fish sauce together to give a thick creamy paste (a food processor may be used). Leave to marinate for 15 minutes. Fill each banana cup with the marinated paste. Put the cups in a steamer for 15-20 minutes. The mixture will rise slightly. When cooked, arrange on a serving plate and garnish each cup with 1 tsp/15ml of thick coconut cream and very thin slivers of red chilli.

FISH CAKES
Tod Man Pla

This recipe makes 16-20 cakes.

5 dried red chillies, deseeded
1 shallot, finely sliced (about 1 tbs/15ml)
2 garlic cloves, chopped (about 1 tbs/15ml)
2 coriander roots, chopped (about 1 tbs/15ml)
small piece galangal, finely chopped (about 1 tbs/15ml)
1 tsp/5ml finely chopped kaffir lime skin or 2 lime leaves, finely chopped
½ tsp/2.5ml salt
1 lb/450 g firm-fleshed fish fillets, without skin and bones, minced/ground (eg. cod, coley, haddock or monkfish)
1 tbs/15ml fish sauce
2 oz/60g thin green/snap beans, sliced *very* fine
oil for deep frying

Using a pestle and mortar or blender, pound the chillies, shallots, garlic, coriander, galangal, kaffir lime skin and salt together into a paste.

Mix the paste thoroughly with the fish, using a pestle and mortar or your hand, making sure all is thoroughly blended. Add the fish sauce and green beans and mix in thoroughly: you should have a firm paste. The best way to achieve this is to knead the mixture with your hand. Shape the mixture into small flat cakes, about 2-2½in/5-6cm in diameter and no more than ½in/1cm thick. Heat the oil to medium hot (the cakes should not fry too quickly or they'll become tough) and deep-fry until golden brown – about 2-3 minutes. Serve with Cucumber relish (see below).

CUCUMBER RELISH

4fl oz/125ml rice vinegar
2 tbs/30ml sugar
2in/5cm piece cucumber (skin left on)
1 small carrot
3 shallots, finely sliced
1 medium chilli, finely sliced
1 tbs/15ml ground roasted peanuts

Boil the sugar and vinegar together until sugar is dissolved and a thin syrup is formed (about 6-7 minutes).

Quarter the cucumber lengthways, then slice finely. Halve the carrot lengthways, then slice finely. Add the cucumber, shallots, carrot, and chilli to the syrup and mix thoroughly. Sprinkle the peanuts on top, stir once and serve.

Fried dough dipped in condensed milk, a snack at the morning market

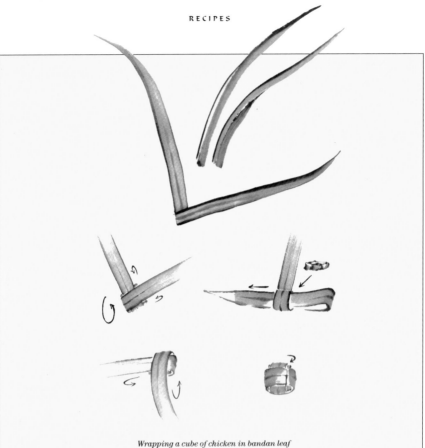

Wrapping a cube of chicken in bandan leaf

CHICKEN WRAPPED IN BANDAN LEAF

Gai Hoh Bai Teoy

The fresh bandan leaf, available from oriental stores, imparts a very delicate flavour, and also makes a very attractive wrapping.

2 tbs/30ml oyster sauce
2 tbs/30ml milk
1 tbs/15ml light soy sauce
1 tbs/15ml sesame oil
2 garlic cloves, finely chopped
8oz/230g boneless chicken, cut in 1in/2.5cm cubes
large pinch of ground white pepper
2 tbs/30ml rice flour
1 young fresh bandan leaf, finely chopped
2 bunches fresh bandan leaves (2 leaves for each cube of meat) about 12in/30cm long
oil for deep frying

Sauce:
5 tbs/75ml rice vinegar
2 tbs/30ml sugar
pinch of salt
1 small red or green chilli, sliced very thin

In a bowl mix the oyster sauce, milk, soy sauce, sesame oil, garlic, pepper, flour and chopped bandan leaf; add the chicken pieces and marinate for at least half an hour. Working with pairs of bandan leaves; place the two leaves at right-angles, overlapping at the angle, and fold them over each other once or twice to make a secure join. Turn over and secure by slipping the last leaf tip into the final fold. Place a cube of meat where the two leaves are joined. Wrap the meat by folding first one then the other leaf around it to make a small package. Secure by slipping the last leaf tip into the final fold.

Make the sauce. In a small pan, boil the

vinegar and sugar together, stirring constantly, until the sugar dissolves and the mixture thickens and starts to brown. Remove from the heat and allow to cool. Add the salt and chilli; stir to mix. Pour into a small bowl.

Steam the pieces of wrapped chicken for about 10 minutes until the leaves are soft. Remove from the steamer. Heat some oil in a deep-fryer and fry the parcels for 5 minutes. Remove and drain. Serve with the sauce.

LITTLE BIRDS
Nok Noy

These chicken 'birds' are a very simple dish, but success depends on your skill with a knife.

6 chicken wings
3 garlic cloves
4 coriander roots
2 tbs/30ml fish sauce
grinding of black pepper
3 tbs/45ml flour
oil for deep frying
Sauce:
8 tbs/120ml rice vinegar
3 tbs/45ml sugar
¼ tsp/1.25ml salt
1 small garlic clove, finely chopped
1 red chilli, finely chopped

From each wing, cut away the wing tip and the first joint (these could be used to make stock). You are now left with the largest, middle, joint. Remove the skin. With a sharp knife, cut between the two parallel bones and separate them at one end. Pull them gently away from each other making sure you don't break the remaining joint. Carefully cut away the meat from the larger bone leaving a small triangle of meat at the tip and fold back over the second bone. The meat will form the body of the 'bird' and the bared bone the neck and head. Gently pierce the meat with a fork. Set aside.

Using a pestle and mortar or blender, pound or blend the garlic with the coriander roots. Turn the mixture into a large bowl, add the fish sauce and black pepper and mix. Add the chicken 'birds' and thoroughly coat them with the mixture. Allow to stand for at least half an hour. Heat the oil in the deep-fryer. Dust the 'birds' in the flour making sure the entire surface of the meat is covered. Fry the 'birds' at medium heat until they are well-browned. Remove from the oil and drain.

Make the sauce. In a small pan, boil together the vinegar and sugar, stirring constantly, until the sugar is dissolved and the mixture starts to thicken. Add the salt, stir, remove from the heat and allow to cool. Add the chopped garlic and chilli, and stir to mix.

Serve in a small bowl to dip the chicken.

Open-air cinema during a temple festival

The author at a market restaurant near the Old Gate, Chiang Mai

FRIED BEEF WITH CRISPY BASIL
Nua Tod Krapow Krob

Deep-frying the fresh sweet basil leaves gives them a beautiful glossy-green colour and adds an interesting texture to this dish.

2 garlic cloves, pounded
3 coriander roots
2 tbs/30ml fish sauce
1 tbs/15ml light soy sauce
1 tsp/5ml sugar
shaking of ground white pepper
6oz/180g lean beef, cut into thin strips
30 sweet basil leaves (without any stalk)
oil for deep frying

Pound the garlic with the coriander, then combine with the fish sauce, soy sauce, sugar and white pepper. Add the beef, stir to ensure that each piece of meat is coated with the mixture, and marinate for at least half an hour.

Heat the oil and deep-fry the meat until slightly crisp at the edges but not too dry. Remove from the oil with a strainer or slotted spoon and turn onto a serving dish. Add the basil leaves to the oil and fry for a few seconds. Remove with a strainer, drain quickly, sprinkle over the beef and serve.

MIXED MEAT AND VEGETABLE CURRY WITH CLEAR NOODLE
Gaeng Ho

Mixed meat and vegetable curry with clear noodle.

8 tbs/125ml/½cup coconut cream
2 tbs/30ml oil
2 garlic cloves, finely chopped
1 tbs/15ml Red curry paste (p. 37)
1 tsp/5ml ground turmeric
3oz/90g boneless chicken, finely sliced
3oz/90g lean pork, finely sliced
2oz/60g dry *Wun Sen* noodles (p. 86), soaked in cold water for 10 minutes to soften (about 4 oz/120g wet weight)
6 tbs/90ml stock/broth or water
2 lime leaves, finely sliced
2 tbs/30ml fish sauce
½ tsp/2.5ml sugar
4-5oz/120-150g mixed prepared vegetables (eg. slivered bamboo shoot, quartered small green aubergines/eggplant, coarsely chopped green/snap beans)
3 long red chillies, finely slivered

In a small pan, warm the coconut cream and reserve. In a wok or frying pan/skillet, heat the oil, add the garlic and fry until golden brown. Add the curry paste and turmeric, stir to mix, and fry together for a few seconds. Add the coconut cream, stir and cook for a few seconds until the mixture starts to thicken and bubble. Add the chicken and pork, stir thoroughly, and cook for a minute or so until you are sure they are cooked through. Add quickly the remaining ingredients, stirring for a second after each addition. Once the chillies have been added, using 2 wooden spoons or similar implements, toss the meats, noodles and vegetables together thoroughly until all are just cooked through. Turn onto a serving dish.

JUNGLE CURRY
Gaeng Pah Moo

This is a very hot dish that can be made with almost any fresh vegetable that is readily available. The distinctive flavour of Krachai (p. 38) is essential to the authenticity of the dish; but if it is unavailable to you, you can still achieve a very tasty curry.

2 tbs/30ml oil
1 garlic clove, finely chopped
1 tbs/15ml Gaeng Pah curry paste (see above right) or Red curry paste (p. 37)
6oz/180g lean pork, finely sliced
approx. 8fl oz/250ml/1cup water
2 tbs/30ml fish sauce
½ tsp/2.5ml sugar
10 slivers of Krachai (p. 38), if using dried, soak in water for 10-15 minutes to soften
4oz/120g prepared vegetables (eg. 6 thin green/ snap beans, trimmed and cut into 1in/2.5cm pieces, 1 small carrot, slivered, 2 small green aubergines/eggplant, quartered)
12-15 holy basil leaves
2 whole green fresh peppercorns, or 15 dried black peppercorns
1 lime leaf, finely chopped
Serves 2

In a wok or frying pan, heat the oil, add the garlic and fry until golden brown. Add the curry paste, stir to mix and fry together for 5-10 seconds. Add the meat, stir to mix and cook for a further 10 seconds, continuing to stir. Add 2 tbs/30ml water, the fish sauce, sugar and the krachai. Stir to mix and cook for a few seconds. Add the vegetables and the remaining water and stir for a few seconds. Add the basil leaves, peppercorns and chopped lime leaf. Stir for a few seconds (the vegetables should retain their crispness). Turn into a bowl and serve.

GAENG PAH CURRY PASTE

8 dried long red chillies, seeded and chopped
4 shallots, chopped
2 garlic cloves, chopped
1 tbs/15ml shrimp paste
1 tsp/5ml finely chopped galangal
1 tbs/15ml chopped lemon grass
1 coriander root, finely chopped
1 tsp/5ml salt
1 tbs/15ml finely chopped krachai

With mortar and pestle or blender, pound or blend all the ingredients together to form a smooth paste.

Nightlife, Patpong Road, Bangkok

RECOMMENDED RESTAURANTS

VIJIT

Democracy Monument,
Rajadamnern Avenue, Bangkok
Telephone 281 6472

A more typically Bangkok restaurant of the old school would be hard to find. The antithesis of 'smart' or fashionable decor, the bland interior is the correct setting for a place that provides unpretentious good cooking for the civil servants and other nearby office workers.

TON KRUANG

120 Sathorn Road, Bangkok
Telephone 234 9663

One of the few 'colonial-style' two-storey wooden houses that have survived the transformation of a once-quiet residential suburb nestling beside a klong, into the city's business centre. A favourite lunch spot for the young and affluent who work in the nearby banks and company headquarters and who expect good food served quickly.

MOON SHADOW

145 Gaysorn Road, Bangkok
Telephone 253 7553

Elegant wooden long-house hung about with antique lamps and other bric-a-brac. Last time I ate at Moon Shadow there was a monsoon downpour which gave me the impression I was eating in a house in the rain-forest; for a moment the city seemed a long way away.

D'JIT POCHANA

1082 Paholyotin Road, Bangkok 9
Telephone 279 5000
60 Sukhumvit Soi 20, Bangkok 11
Telephone 258 1578
23/368-380 Paholyotin Road, Donmuang
(near Airport)
Telephone 531 2716

Thailand's best known and most successful chain of restaurants. Despite the fact that these are food businesses their standards have remained consistently high. You go to D'Jit Pochana because you know exactly what you will get – no risks with the food and a pleasant if unexciting decor. They are the sort of useful restaurants every crowded city needs; and with a branch near to the airport, a boon for the delayed traveller.

Shopping for a meal in the Seafood Market restaurant, Bangkok

SEAFOOD MARKET

388 Sukhumvit Road, Bangkok
Telephone 258 0218

Slightly crazy atmosphere. A cross between a fish warehouse and a cash-and-carry, luridly over-lit and always crowded because it is so bizarre.

TUMNAK THAI

Ruchadapisek Road, Bangkok
Telephone 276 1810

Biggest restaurant in the world! A village of Thai houses offering food from every region of the country. I like to try the North East for a non-Bangkok experience. The waiters on roller-skates add a dash of madness.

BUA

Thanom Liab Menam, Bangkok
Telephone 294 2770

About the best way to spend a last evening in Bangkok. The main restaurant is another of the vast eateries like Tumnak Thai but it is the two-storey boat that offers the best entertainment – a trip on the river as you finish your meal.

RESTAURANTS OUTSIDE BANGKOK

Choosing seafood at the Sang Thai restaurant, Hua Hin

AROON RAI
45 Kojshason Road, Chiang Mai

Scruffy, nondescript street-side restaurant whose food is among the best in Chaing Mai. It is strange that people who put so much effort into making delicious appealing food should care absolutely nothing about the environment in which it is eaten, but that's the way it is.

BAAN SUAN
51/3 Chiang Mai-Sankampaeng Road, Moo 1, Tasala, Chiang Mai
Telephone (053) 242116

Baan Suan, House and Garden, offers good food in an attractive setting – a northern wooden stilt house set in pleasant gardens. Full of charm on a cool upland evening, about four centuries away from the noise and smells of Bangkok.

SANG THAI SEAFOOD
The Harbour, Hua Hin
Telephone 511470

The display of freshly landed produce at the entrance is magical, as is the view of the harbour from the first floor room.

Dicing crispy roast pork served over rice or with noodles for a quick lunch

GLOSSARY

Unhappily, there is no universally agreed system for transcribing Thai words into English. The problem lies in the tonal nature of the Thai language which cannot be expressed easily in European languages. Further, many Thai sounds lie somewhere between two English letters, thus, K and G (the Thai Kuh and Guh sounds) are hard to distinguish. All this has led to an unfortunate mixture of names for Thai dishes in the West with almost no two menus and no two cookery books using the same titles. Regrettably, I have been unable to do any more than add to the confusion by choosing ways to express the Thai names in this book purely on the grounds that they 'seemed right'. The following are some of the Thai cookery terms I have used. You will, I am afraid, need the help of a Thai speaker to fully master their pronunciation.

Ba Mee	Egg noodle	*Moo*	Pork
Cheh	Soak	*Nam Pla*	Fish sauce
Dong	Pickle	*Nam Tan*	Sugar
Gaeng	Soup	*Nua*	Beef
Gaeng Jued	Clear soup	*Nueng*	Steam
Gai	Chicken	*Pad*	Stir-fry
Grat Dook	Spare rib	*Pak*	Vegetables
Gueyteow	Noodles (general)	*Pak Bung*	Swamp cabbage
Gung	Crustacea (prawn/ lobster)	*Pla*	Fish
		Prik	Chilli
Haeng	Dry	*Prik Pon*	Red chilli powder
Kai	Egg	*Puak*	Taro
Karee	Curry	*Saku*	Sago
Kanom	Cake	*Sen Lek*	Wiry or medium rice noodle
Kanom Bang	Bread		
Kem	Salty	*Sen Mee*	Small rice noodle
Khao	Rice	*Sen Yai*	River rice noodle (rice sticks)
Khao Niew	Sticky Rice		
Khao Pad	Fried Rice		
Khao Pohd	Sweet Corn	*Som*	Orange
King	Ginger	*Supparot*	Pineapple
Kong Wan	Desserts (lit: sweet food)	*Tao Hou*	Bean curd
Kratiam	Garlic	*Tod*	Deep-fry
Kruay	Banana	*Tom*	Boil
Lua	Blanch	*Tua*	Bean or nut
		Wun Sen	Vermicelli or clear noodle

A novice monk collecting water

INDEX OF RECIPES BY PRINCIPAL INGREDIENTS

In the order in which they appear in this book

CHICKEN

Fried chicken with bamboo shoots on rice	54
Chicken fried with chilli and nuts	57
Chicken with curry powder	57
Fried rice with chicken and curry powder	62
Chicken, coconut and galangal soup	78
Fried noodles with chicken	87
Fried egg noodles with chicken and bamboo shoots	89
Vermicelli in soup with red bean sauce	90
Red chicken curry	96
Spicy ground meat	140
Chicken with lemon grass curry	146
Chicken satay	163
Golden baskets	192
Wing bean salad	195
Chicken wrapped in Bandan leaf	204
Little birds	205
Mixed meat and vegetable curry with clear noodle	206

PORK

Fried vegetables with pork	56
Pork fried with ginger	56
Vermicelli soup	60
Deep-fried spare-ribs	60
Steamed egg	61
Rice Soup	78
Hot and sour vermicelli salad	80
Steamed spare-ribs with black bean	82
Pork with bamboo shoots	82
Stuffed omelette	83
'Million-year-eggs'	83
River noodles with pork and dark soy	86
Pork and fish ball noodles	86
Pork and vegetable noodle with black beans	89
Fried vermicelli with pork and spring onions	90
Sweet crispy noodle	99
'Ong' pork and chilli sauce	138
Chiang Mai sausage	138
Sausage fried with egg	140
Spicy sausage	140
Sour garlic sausage	141
Skewered marinated pork	141
Chilli soup	142
Chiang Mai curry noodle	142
Chiang Mai curry	143
Stuffed tomatoes	160
Spring rolls	160
Pork sarong	162
Pork toasts	166
Gold bags	166
Jungle curry	207

BEEF

Fried marinated beef	61
Flambéd beef	82
Beef with lime leaves and chilli	82
Minced beef noodle with curry powder	87
Spicy beef noodles with lime leaf	89
Green beef curry	93
Panaeng curry	96
Thai Muslim curry	97
Sliced steak with hot and sour sauce	142
Sliced steak with fried grains of rice in a hot and sour salad	143
Cucumber stuffed with beef	164
Curry noodle	197
Fried beef with crispy basil	206

FISH

Grilled fish with coriander and garlic	113
Steamed fish with ginger and mushrooms	113
Fried fish with pork, ginger and mushrooms	114
Three-flavoured fish	114
Steamed fish with chilli sauce	147
Steamed fish in banana leaf	147
Fish soup with tamarind and ginger	194
Fish with lemon sauce	199
Spicy pickled mud-fish	202
Curried fish steamed in banana leaf	202
Fish cakes	203

PRAWN/SHRIMP/DRIED SHRIMP/ SHRIMP PASTE

Prawn with garlic	56
Pineapple fried rice	63
Fried rice with prawn and chillies	63
Hot and sour soup with prawn	78

The tricky art of turning a stuffed omelette

Nam prik, my mother's style   84
Thai fried noodles   91
Prawn with lemon grass   116
Battered prawns with fresh pickles   117
Prawn with ginger   117
Prawn curry   120
Prawn wrapped in bean curd   164
Prawns in batter with hot and sweet sauce   164
Fried prawn with chilli and lime leaf   198
White radish cake with prawn   198

SQUID

Barbecued seafood   112
Squid with vegetables and oyster sauce   121
Squid with dry curry   122
Stuffed squid soup   122

SHELLFISH

Baby clams in batter with egg and chilli   115
Steamed mussels with lemon grass and
   basil   122
Baby clams with black bean sauce   123
Steamed scallops with garlic   123
Clams with chilli and basil   199
Oysters with red bean curd   199

CRAB/LOBSTER

Hot and sour seafood salad   116
Fried crab claws with curry powder   120
Steamed crab meat   121
Steamed crab claws   121
Crab omelette   123

Bean curd sheet stuffed with crab   194
Grilled lobster with garlic and fresh chilli   199

OTHER

Hot spiced eel   146
Frog with basil leaf   147

VEGETARIAN

Bean curd soup   57
Son-in-law eggs   61
Pickled cabbage   62
Pickled garlic   98
Salty eggs   98
Green papaya salad   143
Sweetcorn cake   163
Hot and sour bamboo salad   195
Young chilli spicy sauce   196
Pak Bung in black bean sauce   196
White radish cake   198
Cucumber relish   203

FRUIT/COOKED DESSERTS

Mango with sticky rice   168
Bananas in syrup   168
Bananas in coconut milk   168
Oranges in syrup   168
Golden threads   169
Coconut custard   172
Baked moong bean and coconut custard   172
Jackfruit seeds   173
Sago with sweetcorn pudding   173
Taro conserve   173

Previous pages: The ruins of Sukhothai,
original capital of the Thai Nation

INDEX

Note: the recipe index is on page 212
Numbers in bold indicate illustrations

Aat, Kuhn 28, 29
Akha, *see Hill Tribes*
American food 74
Andaman Sea, the 21, 103
Aroon Rai, Restaurant **187**
aubergines **37**
Ayuthia, second capital of Siam 19, 21, 77, 152, 190

Ba Klong Dalat, Bangkok Central Market 33, 67
Ba Mee, *see Noodle, egg*
Ba Yon, Chiang Mai charcuterie 131, 134, 135, 138, 186
Baan Suan, Restaurant **178**, 187
Baht, Currency of Thailand 70
Ban Chiang, culture, pottery 135
banana leaf **37**
bandan leaf 204
Bangkok, capital of Thailand 18, 19, 21, 24, 28, 42, 46, 49, 66, 77, 102, 105, 126, 128, 130, 134, 135, 136, 150, 152, 157, 180, 189, 190
Bangkok Bank, The 75
basil **37**
bean curd **37**
bean curd sheets **37**
bean sauce 37
Bhumichitr, Aw, author's sister-in-law 158, 159
Bhumichitr, Ed, author's brother 48
Bhumichitr, Ooie, author's brother 157, 158, 159
Bhumiphol Adulyadej, Rama IX, present King of Thailand 24, 52, 136, 152, 153, 157
Bodh Gaya, Indian Temple 126
breakfast, Thai style 74, 78
broth, *see stock*
Brynner, Yul 18, 151
Buddhism:
    monks 18, 24, 48, 157
    monuments 109, 152
    practice of 71, 152
    spread of from Sri Lanka 19
Bua, Restaurant 190
Bua Tong, Restaurant 190

Burma 18, 126, 152, 187

Cambodia 18, 135
carambola, *see Star Fruit*
carving, vegetables **174**
Cha'am, beach resort 104
Chakri, ruling dynasty of Thailand 21, 129, 152
Chan, Khun, Royal vegetable carver 153, 176
Chao Phya, principal river of Thailand 19, 21, 28, 33, 46, 53, 66, 190
Chao Phya Chakri, King of Siam 21, 66
Chi Po, *see Preserved turnip*
Chiang Mai, City of 126, 127, 129, 134, 135, 136, 187
Chiang Mai, Kingdom of 21
Chiang Mai, Restaurant, London 14, 181, 190
chillies **34**, 128
Chinese, community in Thailand 21, 28, 53, 67, 68, 75, 180, 182
Chitrilada Palace, private residence of Thai monarch 136, 153
Chulalongkorn, King Rama V of Siam 22, 41, 180
City of Angels, *see Bangkok*
coconut **34**
coriander **34**
curry, paste and powder **37, 92**

Democracy Monument 180, **181**
desserts **168, 169**
D'jit Pochana, Thai restaurant chain 187
durian, tropical fruit 156

eggplant *see aubergines*
Emerald Buddha, Temple of 66, 151, 152
Erewan, Hotel and Shrine 71
First World War 102
fish, preparation of **110**
    types of **112**
fish sauce **34**
fragrant rice *see rice*
French Indo-China 18
Friendship Highway, American military road 135
fruit, Thai, tropical **167**

galanga *see galangal*
galangal **38**
galangale *see galangal*
garlic **34**
Gaysorn, district of Bangkok 183
Gee, family 129, 137
ginger **38**
Golden Mount, Bangkok **71**, 77
Golden Triangle, the 21, 126
Grand Palace, Bangkok 52, 66, 75, 153, 180
Guinness Book of Records 190
Gulf of Thailand 21, 102
Hill Tribes 126, 136, 137
Hinduism 19, 52, 74
Hmong, *see Hill Tribes*
Hua Hin, beach resort 102, 104, 105, 109, 135, 150, 187, 189
Hua Ta Keh, market town 46

Indian market, Bangkok 76
Issan, people of North-Eastern Thailand 135

kaffir lime **38**
kang kung, *see Swamp cabbage*
Karen, *see Hill Tribes*
kha, *see galangal*
Khao Luang Cave, near Phetchaburi 151
khan toke, Northern traditional dinner 137
Khmer 18, 134
Killing Fields, The, film 104
King and I, The, film 151
Klai Kangwan, Royal villa 102
Klong Tuey, Bangkok Harbour 53, 191
Koh Samet 103
Koh Samui 103
Korat, city of 13, 135, 136
krachai **38**
Krung Thep, *see Bangkok*
Kwai, River, Bridge over the 23

Lahmdoun, Chiang Mai restaurant 130
Lahu, *see Hill Tribes*
Lakom, Thai classical dance 180
Laos 18, 21, 126
Laos root, *see galangal*
lemon grass **36**
Leonowens, Anna, English author 151
lime leaves **36**
Lisu, *see Hill Tribes*

look choob 158
Lord of Life, *see Chakri Dynasty*
Loy Krathong, Thai festival 53
Lumpini Park 68
lychee 167

Mae Sae Valley, holiday resort 127, 128, 137
Mahidol, Ananda, Rama VIII **150**
Malaysia (Malaya) 18, 28, 102, 103
mango 167
mangosteen 167
Marco Polo 85
measurements **43**
Mekong River 135
Mekong, Thai whisky 42, 183
Mongkut, King Rama IV of Siam 22, 150, 151
Mongkut, King, Institute of Technology 48
Moon Shadow, restaurant 182, 183
mushrooms **38**, 126, 128, 137

nam maw, fermented sausage 134
noodles 41, 75, **85**
  cellophane 86
  egg 85
  medium flat 85
  rice vermicelli 86
  river, rice 85

oil **36**
Old Chiang Mai cultural centre 137
opium 126, 136
Oriental Hotel, the 190
Oriental Queen, restaurant 190
oyster sauce **38**

Pagan, Burmese temple 126
pak bung, *see Swamp cabbage*
Patpong Road, Bangkok red-light district 186
Pattaya, beach resort 102, 103, 104
peanuts **38**
pepper **36**
Phangnga Bay 103
Phetchaburi, regional capital 150, 151, 152
Phnom Penh Hotel, *see Railway Hotel*

Phuket, southern island 103, 189
Pimai, Khmer temple 135
ploughing ceremony 52
Pra Poom, spirit of the land 71, 74, 156
Pramane Ground, Bangkok 52
Pratuname, Bangkok market 77
preserved radish 39
preserved turnip 38

Railway Hotel, the, Hua Hin 102, 104, 105
Rama I, King, see Chao Phya Chakri
Rama VI, King 68, 104
Rama VII, King 102, 109
Rambaibani, Queen of Thailand 129
rambutan 167
Ramkamhaeng, Second King of Sukhothai
   19
Rayong 103
red bean curd 37
rice 54
rice vinegar 39
rice sticks, see River rice noodle
Rim Nam, restaurant 190
river rice noodle 85
Royal Barge procession 67

Saladaeng, suburb of Bangkok 28
samloh, bicycle rickshaw 105
Sang Thai, restaurant 187, 189, 209
Sathorn Klong, canal in Bangkok 28, 182
scallion, see Spring onion
seafood, preparation of 110
Seafood Market, restaurant 189, 208
sen lek, see Noodle, medium flat
sen mee, see Noodle, rice vermicelli
sen yai, see River rice noodle
shallots 39
Shell (Thai) Good Food Guide 187
shrimp, dried 38
   paste 39
Si Satchenali, village in Central Thailand 157
Siamese Princess, restaurant 190
Singha, Thai beer 42
Sirikit, Queen of Thailand 136, 152
Sofitel, French hotel chain 105

Som Jai, leading Thai cook 186, 187
Sometime, restaurant 183
soy sauce 36
spring onion 39
star fruit 167
steaming 40
sticky rice 128, 134, 137
stir frying 40
stock 40
Sukhothai, early Siamese capital 18, 19, 46
swamp cabbage 196

Taksin, General and first King of modern
   Siam 21, 66
tamarind 39
tang chi, see preserved radish
taro 39
Thai Inter, national airline 156
Thonburi, town, suburb of modern Bangkok
   21, 66
Tilokaraje, King of Chiang Mai 126
Ton Kruang, restaurant 182
tuctuc, motorised rickshaw 67
Tumnak Thai, restaurant 184/5, 190
turmeric 39

vegetable carving, see carving
Vietnam War 23, 135, 183
Vijit, restaurant 180, 181
Vimanmek, the, Royal Palace 41, 180

Wararot, Chiang Mai food market 135
Wat Arun, Temple of the Dawn 66, 67
Wat Chet Yot, Chiang Mai temple 126, 127
Wat Fa Ham, Chiang Mai temple 130
Wat Mahathat, Phetchaburi temple 152
water convolvulus, see Swamp cabbage
wun sen, see Noodles, cellophane

Yasothan rocket festival 150
Yowarat, Bangkok's Chinatown 75, 76

PHOTOGRAPHIC ACKNOWLEDGEMENTS

Location photographs unless listed here
are by Michael Freeman
Recipe photographs are by Clive Streeter
Line illustrations are by Jane Evans
(Virgil Pomfret Agency)

The remaining photographs are reproduced by
kind permission of the following:

BBC Hulton Picture Library: p17 (King Mongkut 1868),
p19 (Suburban letter box 1911), p46 (House on a klong),
p102 (Prince Chula 1952), p150 (Ananda Mahidol, King of Siam 1925-1946)

Mary Evans Picture Library: pp28, 66

The Mansell Collection: p18

Photobank: p52 (The Ploughing Ceremony),
p65 (Early XIX Century Thai lacquer design),
p126 (King Rama VII enters Chiang Mai),
p188 (A Remekein show with foodstalls in the foreground
in the time of King Rama V)